LAST
CHANCE
TO SEE

LAST
CHANCE
TO SEE

DOUGLAS ADAMS
AND
MARK CARWARDINE

HARMONY BOOKS
NEW YORK

Published by Harmony Books, 201 East 50th Street, New York, New York
10022. Member of the Crown Publishing Group.
Originally published in Great Britain by William Heinemann Ltd. in 1990.

HARMONY and colophon are trademarks of Crown Publishers, Inc.

Manufactured in the United States of America

Library of Congress Cataloging-in-Publication Data

Adams, Douglas, 1952–
Last chance to see / Douglas Adams and Mark Carwardine.
p.   cm.
1. Endangered species. 2. Adams, Douglas, 1952–   —Journeys.
3. Carwardine, Mark—Journeys. I. Carwardine, Mark. II. Title.
QL82.A33   1991
591.52′9—dc20   90-42756
CIP

Design by John Fontana

FOR ALAIN LE GARSMEUR

Contents

Preface

This book is about a series of journeys that Mark Carwardine and I went on to look for some of the world's rarest and most endangered animals, and one or two that aren't quite so endangered but will be pretty soon if we don't watch out. The trip to Madagascar was in 1985, and the others were made over a period of about ten months in 1988 and 1989.

The photographer Alain le Garsmeur came with us to Madagascar, but we were unable to persuade him to give up the best part of a year to come with us on the other trips, so Mark and I took all the photographs in this book. Any of them that are any good are so as a result of Alain's advice, help, and enthusiasm. Any that aren't as good as they should be would have been better if he'd been there to take them himself.

All the trips, other than the one to Madagascar, were recorded for BBC Radio. The producer of the series was Gaynor Shutte. She came with us to Indonesia and New Zealand to record us in the field and make sure that we basically knew what we were doing. Chris Muir was the sound recordist in Zaïre and China, and Stephen Faux recorded us in Mauritius.

Mark did the tough bits. He did all the preparation and organisation and research involved in mounting the trips, and also taught me most of the small amount I now know about zoology, ecology, and conservation work. All I had to do was turn up with a suitcase and try to remember what happened for long enough afterward to write it down.

Douglas Adams

LAST
CHANCE
TO SEE

TWIG
TECHNOLOGY

HIS ISN'T AT ALL
what I expected. In 1985, by some sort of journalistic acci-
dent, I was sent to Madagascar with Mark Carwardine to
look for an almost extinct form of lemur called the aye-aye.
None of the three of us had met before. I had never met
Mark, Mark had never met me, and no one, apparently, had
seen an aye-aye in years.

This was the idea of the *Observer Colour Magazine,* to
throw us all in at the deep end. Mark is an extremely experienced and knowledgeable zoologist who was working at
that time for the World Wildlife Fund, and his role, essentially, was to be the one who knew what he was talking
about. My role, and one for which I was entirely qualified,
was to be an extremely ignorant non-zoologist to whom
everything that happened would come as a complete sur-

prise. All the aye-aye had to do was do what aye-ayes have been doing for millions of years; sit in a tree and hide.

The aye-aye is a nocturnal lemur. It is a very strange-looking creature that seems to have been assembled from bits of other animals. It looks a little like a large cat with a bat's ears, a beaver's teeth, a tail like a large ostrich feather, a middle finger like a long dead twig, and enormous eyes that seem to peer past you into a totally different world which exists just over your left shoulder.

Like virtually everything that lives on Madagascar, it does not exist anywhere else on earth. Its origins date back to a period in earth's history when Madagascar was still part of mainland Africa (which itself had been part of the gigantic supercontinent of Gondwanaland), at which time the ancestors of the Madagascan lemurs were the dominant primate in all the world. When Madagascar sheered off into the Indian Ocean, it became entirely isolated from all the evolutionary changes that took place in the rest of the world. It is a life raft from a different time. It is now almost like a tiny, fragile, separate planet.

The major evolutionary change that passed Madagascar by was the arrival of the monkeys. These were descended from the same ancestors as the lemurs, but they had bigger brains, and were aggressive competitors for the same habitat. Where the lemurs had been content to hang around in trees having a good time, the monkeys were ambitious, and interested in all sorts of things, especially twigs, with which they found they could do all kinds of things that they couldn't do by themselves—dig for things, probe things, hit things. The monkeys took over the world and the lemur branch of the primate family died out everywhere—other than on Madagascar, which for millions of years the monkeys never reached.

Then fifteen hundred years ago, the monkeys finally arrived, or at least the monkeys' descendants—us. Thanks to astounding advances in twig technology, we arrived in ca-

2
▼▼▼

noes, then boats, and finally airplanes, and once again started to compete for use of the same habitat, only this time with fire and machetes and domesticated animals, with asphalt and concrete. The lemurs are once again fighting for survival.

My airplane full of monkey descendants arrived at Antananarivo airport. Mark, who had gone out ahead to make the arrangements for the expedition, met me for the first time there and explained the setup.

"Everything's gone wrong," he said.

He was tall, dark, and laconic and had a slight nervous tic. He explained that he used to be just tall, dark, and laconic, but that the events of the last few days had rather got to him. At least he tried to explain this. He had lost his voice, he croaked, due to a lot of recent shouting.

"I nearly telexed you not to come," he said. "The whole thing's a nightmare. I've been here for five days and I'm still waiting for something to go right. The Ambassador in Brussels promised me that the Ministry of Agriculture would be able to provide us with two Landrovers and a helicopter. Turns out all they've got is a moped and it doesn't work.

"The Ambassador in Brussels also assured me that we could drive right to the north, but the road suddenly turns out to be impassable because it's being rebuilt by the Chinese, only we're not supposed to know that. And exactly what is meant by 'suddenly' I don't know because they've apparently been at it for ten years.

"Anyway, I think I've managed to sort something out, but we have to hurry," he added. "The plane to the jungle leaves in two hours and we have to be on it. We've just got time to dump your surplus baggage at the hotel if we're quick. Er, some of it is surplus, isn't it?" He looked anxiously at the pile of bags that I was lugging, and then with increasing alarm at the cases of Nikon camera bodies, lenses, and tripods that our photographer, Alain le Garsmeur, who had been with me on the plane, was busy loading into the minibus.

"Oh, that reminds me," Mark said, "I've just found out that we probably won't be allowed to take any film out of the country."

I climbed rather numbly into the minibus. After thirteen hours on the plane from Paris, I was tired and disoriented and had been looking forward to a shower, a shave, a good night's sleep, and then maybe a gentle morning trying gradually to find Madagascar on the map over a pot of tea. I tried to pull myself together and get a grip. I suddenly had not the faintest idea what I, a writer of humorous science-fiction adventures, was doing here. I sat blinking in the glare of the tropical sun and wondered what on earth Mark was expecting of me. He was hurrying around, tipping one porter, patiently explaining to another porter that he hadn't actually carried any of our bags, conducting profound negotiations with the driver, and gradually pulling some sort of order out of the chaos.

Madagascar, I thought. Aye-aye, I thought. A nearly extinct lemur. Heading out to the jungle in two hours' time. I desperately needed to sound bright and intelligent.

4
▼▼▼

"Er, do you think we're actually going to get to see this animal?" I asked Mark as he climbed in and slammed the door. He grinned at me.

"Well, the Ambassador in Brussels said we haven't got a hope in hell," he said, "so we may just be in with a chance. Welcome," he added as we started the slow pothole slalom into town, "to Madagascar."

Antananarivo is pronounced *Tananarive,* and for much of this century was spelled that way as well. When the French took over Madagascar at the end of the last century ("colonised" is probably too kind a word for moving in on a country that was doing perfectly well for itself but which the French simply took a fancy to), they were impatient with the curious Malagasy habit of not bothering to pronounce the first and last syllables of place names. They decided, in their rational Gallic way, that if that was how the names were pronounced, then they could damn well be spelt that way too. It would be as if someone had taken over England and told us that from now on we would be spelling Leicester "Lester" and liking it. We might be forced to spell it that way, but we wouldn't like it, and neither did the Malagasy. As soon as they managed to divest themselves of French rule, in the 1960s, they promptly reinstated all the old spellings and just kept the cooking and the bureaucracy.

One of the more peculiar things that has happened to me is that as a result of an idea I had as a penniless hitchhiker sleeping in fields and telephone boxes, publishers now send me around the world on expensive author tours and put me up in the sort of hotel room where you have to open several doors before you find the bed. In fact, I was arriving in Antananarivo directly from a U.S. author tour which was exactly like that, and so my first reaction to finding myself sleeping on concrete floors in spider-infested huts in the middle of the jungle was, oddly enough, one of fantastic relief. Weeks of mind-numbing American Expressness dropped away like mud in the shower and I was able to lie back and enjoy being wonderfully, serenely, hideously uncomfortable. I could tell that Mark didn't realise this and was at first rather anxious showing me to my patch of floor—"Er, will this be all right? I was told there would be mattresses. . . . Um, can we fluff up the concrete a little for you?"—and I had to keep on saying, "You don't understand. This is great, this is wonderful, I've been looking forward to this for weeks."

In fact, we were not able to lie back at all. The aye-aye is a nocturnal animal and does not make daytime appointments. The few aye-ayes that were known to exist in 1985 were to be found (or more usually not found) on a tiny, idyllic, rain-forest island called Nosy Mangabé, just off the northeast coast of Madagascar to which they had been re-

5
▼▼▼

moved twenty years earlier. This was their last refuge on earth and no one was allowed to visit the island without special government permission, which Mark had managed to arrange for us. This was where our hut was, and this was where we spent night after night thrashing through the rain forest in torrential rain carrying tiny feeble torches (the big powerful ones we'd brought on the plane stayed with the "surplus" baggage we'd dumped in the Antananarivo Hilton) until . . . we found the aye-aye.

That was the extraordinary thing. We actually did find the creature. We only caught a glimpse of it for a few seconds, slowly edging its way along a branch a couple of feet above our heads and looking down at us through the rain with a sort of serene incomprehension as to what kind of things we might possibly be, but it was the kind of moment about which it is hard not to feel completely dizzy.

Why?

Because, I realised later, I was a monkey looking at a lemur.

By flying from New York and Paris to Antananarivo by 747 jet, up to Diégo-Suarez in an old prop plane, driving to the port of Maroantsetra in an even older truck, crossing to Nosy Mangabé in a boat that was so old and dilapidated it was almost indistinguishable from driftwood, and finally walking by night into the ancient rain forest, we were almost making a time journey back through all the stages of our experiments in twig technology to the environment from which we had originally ousted the lemurs. And here was one of the very last of them, looking at me with, as I say, serene incomprehension.

The following day, Mark and I sat on the steps of the hut in the morning sunshine making notes and discussing ideas for the article I would write for the *Observer* about the expedition. He had explained to me in detail the history of lemurs and I said that I thought there was an irony to it.

Madagascar had been a monkey-free refuge for the lemurs off the coast of mainland Africa, and now Nosy Mangabé had to be a monkey-free refuge off the coast of mainland Madagascar. The refuges were getting smaller and smaller, and the monkeys were already here on this one, sitting making notes about it.

"The difference," said Mark, "is that the first monkey-free refuge was set up by chance. The second was actually set up by the monkeys."

"So I suppose it's fair to say that as our intelligence has increased, it has given us not only greater power, but also an understanding of the consequences of using that power. It has given us the ability to control our environment, but also the ability to control ourselves."

"Well, up to a point," said Mark, "up to a point. There are twenty-one species of lemur on Madagascar now, of which the aye-aye is thought to be the rarest, which just means that it's the one that's currently closest to the edge. At one time there were over forty. Nearly half of them have been pushed over the edge already. And that's just the lemurs. Virtually everything that lives in the Madagascan rain forest doesn't live anywhere else at all, and there's only about ten percent of that left. And that's just Madagascar. Have you ever been to mainland Africa?"

"No."

"One species after another is on the way out. And they're really major animals. There are less than twenty northern white rhino left, and there's a desperate battle going on to save them from the poachers. They're in Zaïre. And the mountain gorillas too—they're one of man's closest living relatives, but we've almost killed them off this century. And it's happening throughout the rest of the world as well. Do you know about the kakapo?"

"The what?"

"The kakapo. It's the world's largest, fattest, and least-

7
▼▼▼

able-to-fly parrot. It lives in New Zealand. It's the strangest bird I know of and will probably be as famous as the dodo when it goes extinct."

"How many of them are there?"

"Forty and falling. Do you know about the Yangtze river dolphin?"

"No."

"The Komodo dragon? The Rodrigues fruit bat?"

"Wait a minute, wait a minute," I said. I went into the hut and rummaged around in the ants for one of the monkey's most prized achievements. It consisted of a lot of twigs mashed up to a pulp, flattened out into sheets, and then held together with something that had previously held a cow together. I took my Filofax outside and flipped through it while the sun streamed through the trees behind me from which some ruffed lemurs were calling to one another.

"Well," I said, sitting down on the step again, "I've just got a couple of novels to write, but, er, what are you doing in 1988?"

HERE BE CHICKENS

HE FIRST ANIMAL
we went to look for, three years later, was the Komodo
dragon lizard. This was an animal, like most of the animals
we were going to see, about which I knew very little. What
little I did know was hard to like.

They are man-eaters. That is not so bad in itself. Lions and
tigers are man-eaters, and though we may be intensely wary
of them and treat them with respectful fear, we nevertheless
have an instinctive admiration for them. We don't actually
like to be eaten by them, but we don't resent the very idea.
The reason, probably, is that we are mammals and so are
they. There's a kind of unreconstructed species prejudice at
work: a lion is one of us but a lizard is not. And neither, for
that matter, is a fish, which is why we have such an unholy
terror of sharks.

The Komodo lizards are also big. Very big. There's one on Komodo at the moment which is over twelve feet long and stands about a yard high, which you can't help but feel is entirely the wrong size for a lizard to be, particularly if it's a man-eater and you're about to go and share an island with it.

Though they are man-eaters, they don't get to eat man very often, and more generally their diet consists of goats, pigs, deer, and such like, but they will only kill these animals if they can't find something that's dead already, because they are, at heart, scavengers. They like their meat bad and smelly. We don't like our meat like that and tend to be leery of things that do. I was definitely leery of these lizards.

Mark had spent part of the intervening three years planning and researching the expeditions we were to make, writing letters, telephoning, but most often telexing to naturalists working in the field in remote parts of the world, organising schedules, letters of introduction, and maps. He also arranged all the visas, flights and boats, and accommodation, and then had to arrange them all over again when it turned out that I hadn't quite finished the novels yet.

At last they were done. I left my house in the hands of the builders, who claimed they only had three more weeks' work to do, and set off to fulfill my one last commitment—an author tour of Australia. I'm always very sympathetic when I hear people complaining that all they ever get on television or radio chat shows is authors honking on about their latest book. It does, on the other hand, get us out of the house and spare our families the trial of hearing us honking on about our latest book.

Finally that too was over and we could start looking for giant lizards.

We met up in a hotel room in Melbourne and examined our array of expeditionary equipment. "We" were Mark,

myself, and Gaynor Shutte, a BBC producer who was going to be recording our exploits for a radio documentary series. Our equipment was a vast array of cameras, tape recorders, tents, sleeping bags, medical supplies, mosquito coils, unidentifiable things made of canvas and nylon with metal eyelets and plastic hooks, windbreakers, boots, penknives, torches, and a cricket bat.

None of us would admit to having brought the cricket bat. We couldn't understand what it was doing there. We phoned room service to bring us up some beers and also to take the cricket bat away, but they didn't want it. The guy from room service said that if we were really going to look for man-eating lizards, maybe the cricket bat would be a handy thing to have.

"If you find you've got a dragon charging toward you at thirty miles an hour snapping its teeth, you can always drive it defensively through the covers," he said, deposited the beers and left.

We hid the cricket bat under the bed, opened the beers, and let Mark explain something of what we were in for.

"For centuries," he said, "the Chinese told stories of great scaly man-eating monsters with fiery breath, but they were thought to be nothing more than myths and fanciful imaginings. Old sailors would tell of them, and would write 'Here be dragons' on their maps when they saw a land they didn't at all like the look of.

"And then, at the beginning of this century, a pioneering Dutch visitor was attempting to island-hop his way along the Indonesian archipelago to Australia when he had engine trouble and had to crash-land his plane on the tiny island of Komodo. He survived the crash but his plane didn't.

"He went to search for water. As he was searching, he found a strange wide track on the sandy shore, followed the track, and suddenly found himself confronted with something that he, also, didn't at all like the look of. It appeared

to be a great scaly man-eating monster, fully ten feet long. What he was looking at was the thing we are going to look for—the Komodo dragon lizard."

"Did he survive?" I asked, going straight for the point.

"Yes, he did, though his reputation didn't. He stayed alive for three months, and then was rescued. But when he went home, everyone thought he was mad and nobody believed a word of it."

"So were the Komodo dragons the origin of the Chinese dragon myths?"

"Well, nobody really knows, of course. At least I don't. But it certainly seems like a possibility. It's a large creature with scales, it's a man-eater, and though it doesn't actually breathe fire, it does have the worst breath of any creature known to man. But there's something else you should know about the island as well."

"What?"

"Have another beer first."

I did.

"There are," said Mark, "more poisonous snakes per square metre of ground on Komodo than on any equivalent area on earth."

There is in Melbourne a man who probably knows more about poisonous snakes than anyone else on earth. His name is Dr. Struan Sutherland, and he has devoted his entire life to a study of venom.

"And I'm bored with it," he said when we went along to see him the next morning. "Can't stand all these poisonous creatures, all these snakes and insects and fish and things. Stupid things, biting everybody. And then people expect me to tell them what to do about it. I'll tell them what to do. Don't get bitten in the first place. That's the answer. I've had enough of it. Hydroponics, now, *that's* interesting. Talk to you all you like about hydroponics. Fascinating stuff, growing plants artificially in water, very interesting technique.

We'll need to know all about it if we're going to go to Mars and places. Where did you say you were going?"

"Komodo."

"Well, don't get bitten, that's all I can say. And don't come running to me if you do because you won't get here in time, and anyway I'll probably be out. Hate this office, look at it. Full of poisonous animals all over the place. Look at this tank, it's full of fire ants. Poisonous. Bored silly with them. Anyway, I got some little cakes in in case you were hungry. Would you like some little cakes? I can't remember where I put them. There's some tea but it's not very good. Sit down for heaven's sake.

"So, you're going to Komodo. Well, I don't know why you want to do that, but I suppose you have your reasons. There are fifteen different types of snake on Komodo, and half of them are poisonous. The only potentially deadly ones are the Russell's viper, the bamboo viper, and the Indian cobra.

"The Indian cobra is the fifteenth deadliest snake in the world, and all the other fourteen are here in Australia. That's why it's so hard for me to find time to get on with my hydroponics, with all these snakes all over the place.

"And spiders. The most poisonous spider is the Sydney funnel web, which bites about five hundred people a year. A lot of them used to die, so I had to develop an antidote to stop people bothering me with it all the time. Took us years. Then we developed this snake-bite detector kit. Not that you need a kit to tell you when you've been bitten by a snake, you usually know, but the kit is something that will detect what you've been bitten by so you can treat it properly.

"Would you like to see a kit? I've got a couple in the venom fridge. Let's have a look. Ah, look, the cakes are in here too. Quick, have one while they're still fresh. Fairy cakes, I baked 'em myself."

He handed around the snake-bite detectors kits and the rock-hard fairy cakes and retreated back to his desk, where he beamed at us cheerfully from behind his curly beard and

13
▼▼▼

bow tie. We admired the kits more than the cakes and asked him how many of the snakes he had been bitten by himself.

"None of 'em," he said. "Another area of expertise I've developed is that of getting other people to handle the dangerous animals. Won't do it myself. Don't want to get bitten, do I? You know what it says in my entry in *Who's Who?* 'Hobbies: gardening—with gloves; fishing—with boots; traveling—with care.' That's the answer. Oh, and wear baggy trousers. When a snake strikes, it starts to inject venom as soon as it hits something. If you've got baggy trousers, most of the venom will just get squirted down the inside of your trousers, which is better than it being squirted down the inside of your leg. You're not eating your cakes. Come on, get them down you, there's plenty more in the fridge."

We asked, tentatively, if we could perhaps take a snakebite detector kit with us to Komodo.

" 'Course you can, 'course you can. Take as many as you like. Won't do you a blind bit of good because they're only for Australian snakes."

"So what do we do if we get bitten by something deadly, then?" I asked.

He blinked at me as if I were stupid.

"Well, what do you think you do?" he said. "You die, of course. That's what deadly means."

"But what about cutting open the wound and sucking out the poison?" I asked.

"Rather you than me," he said. "I wouldn't want a mouthful of poison. All the blood vessels beneath the tongue are very close to the surface, so the poison goes straight into the bloodstream. That's assuming you could get much of the poison out, which you probably couldn't. And in a place like Komodo it means you'd quickly have a seriously infected wound to contend with as well as a leg full of poison. Septicemia, gangrene, you name it. It'll kill you."

"What about a tourniquet?"

"Fine if you don't mind having your leg off afterwards.

You'd have to because it would be dead. And if you can find anyone in that part of Indonesia who you'd trust to take your leg off, then you're a braver man than me. No, I'll tell you: the only thing you can do is apply a pressure bandage direct to the wound and wrap the whole leg up tightly, but not too tightly. Slow the blood flow but don't cut it off or you'll lose the leg. Keep the leg, or whatever bit of you it is you've been bitten in, lower than your heart and your head. Keep very, very still, breathe slowly, and get to a doctor *immediately*. If you're on Komodo, though, that means a couple of days, by which time you'll be well dead. "The only answer, and I mean this quite seriously, is *don't get bitten*. There's no reason why you should. Any of the snakes there will get out of your way well before you even see them. You don't really need to worry about the snakes if you're careful. No, the things you really need to worry about are the marine creatures."

"What?"

"Scorpion fish, stonefish, sea snakes. Much more poisonous than anything on land. Get stung by a stonefish and the pain alone can kill you. People drown themselves just to stop the pain."

"Where are all these things?"

"Oh, just in the sea. Tons of them. I wouldn't go near it if I were you. Full of poisonous animals. Hate them."

"Is there anything you do like?"

"Hydroponics."

"No, I mean is there any venomous creature you're particularly fond of?"

He looked out of the window for a moment.

"There was," he said, "but she left me."

We flew to Bali.

David Attenborough has said that Bali is the most beautiful place in the world, but he must have been there longer than we were, and seen different bits, because most of what

15
▼▼▼

we saw in the couple of days we were there sorting out our travel arrangements was awful. It was just the tourist area, i.e., that part of Bali which has been made almost exactly the same as everywhere else in the world for the sake of people who have come all this way to see Bali.

The narrow, muddy streets of Kuta were lined with gift shops and hamburger bars and populated with crowds of drunken, shouting tourists, Kamikaze motorcyclists, counterfeit-watch sellers, and small dogs. The kamikaze motorcyclists tried to pick off the tourists and the small dogs, while the tiny minibus which we spent most of the evening in shuttling our bags from one full hotel to another, hurtled through the motorcyclists and counterfeit-watch sellers at video-game speeds. Somewhere not too far from here, toward the middle of the island, there may have been heaven on earth, but hell had certainly set up business on its porch.

The tourists with their cans of lager and their FUCK OFF T-shirts were particularly familiar to anyone who has seen the English at play in Spain or Greece, but I suddenly realised as I watched this that for once I didn't need to hide myself away in embarrassment. They weren't English. They were Australian.

But they were otherwise so nearly identical that it started me thinking about convergent evolution, which I had better explain before I go on to say why they made me think of it.

In different parts of the world, strikingly similar but completely unrelated forms of life will emerge in response to similar conditions and habitats. For instance, the aye-aye, the lemur that Mark and I originally tracked down in Madagascar, has one particularly remarkable feature. Its third finger is much longer than its other fingers and is skeletally thin, almost like a twig. It uses this finger for poking around under the bark of the trees it lives in to dig out the grubs which it feeds on.

There is one other creature in the world which does this, and that is the long-fingered possum, which is found in New

Guinea. It has a long and skeletally thin fourth finger, which it uses for precisely the same purpose. There is no family relationship between these two animals at all, and the only common factor between them is this: an absence of woodpeckers.

There are no woodpeckers in Madagascar, and no woodpeckers in Papua New Guinea. This means that there is a food source—the grubs under the bark—going free, and in these two cases it is a mammal that has developed a mechanism for getting at it. And the mechanism they both use is the same—different finger, same idea. But it is purely the selection process of evolution that has created this similarity, because the animals themselves are not related.

Exactly the same behaviour pattern had emerged entirely independently on the other side of the world. As in the gift shop habitats of Spain or Greece, or indeed Hawaii, the local people cheerfully offer themselves up for insult and abuse in return for money which they then spend on further despoiling their habitat to attract more money-bearing predators.

17
▼▼▼

"Right," said Mark, when the three of us found some dinner that night in a tourist restaurant with plastic flowers and Muzak and paper umbrellas in the drinks, "here's the picture. We have to get a goat."

"Here?" asked Gaynor.

"No. In Labuan Bajo. Labuan Bajo is on the island of Flores and is the nearest port to Komodo. It's a crossing of about twenty-two miles across some of the most treacherous seas in the East. This is where the South China Sea meets the Indian Ocean, and it's riddled with crosscurrents, riptides, and whirlpools. It's very dangerous and could take anything up to twenty hours."

"With a *goat*?" I asked.

"A dead goat."

I toyed with my food.

"It's best," continued Mark, "if the goat has been dead for

about three days, so it's got a good smell going. That's more likely to attract the dragons."

"You're proposing twenty hours on a boat—"

"A small boat," added Mark.

"On violently heaving seas—"

"Probably."

"With a three-day-old dead goat."

"Yes."

"I hardly know what to say."

"There's one other thing that I should probably say, which is that I've no idea if any of this is true. There are wildly conflicting stories, and some are probably just out of date, or even completely made up. I hope we'll have a better idea of the situation when we get to Labuan Bajo tomorrow. We're flying tomorrow, via Bima, and we should be at Denpasar airport early. It was a nightmare getting these tickets and the connecting flight, and we *mustn't* miss the plane."

18
▼▼▼

We did. Fresh eruptions of hell awaited us at Denpasar airport, which was a turmoil of crowds and shouting, with a sense of incipient violence simmering just beneath the surface. The airline check-in man said that our flight from Bima to Labuan Bajo had not been confirmed by the travel agent and as a result we had no seats. He shrugged and gave us back our tickets.

We had been told that serenity was the best frame of mind with which to tackle Indonesia and we decided to try it. We tried serenely to point out that it actually said "Confirmed" on our tickets, but he explained that "Confirmed" didn't actually mean *confirmed*, as such, it was merely something that they wrote on tickets when people asked them to because it saved a lot of bother and made them go away.

He went away.

We stood waggling our tickets serenely at thin air. Behind the check-in desk was a window, and behind this a thin airline official with a thin moustache, a thin tie, and a white shirt with thin epaulets sat smoking cigarettes and staring at us impassively through narrow wreaths of smoke. We waved our tickets at him, but he just shook his head very, very slightly.

We marched serenely over to the ticket office, where they said it was nothing to do with them, we should talk to the travel agent. A number of decreasingly serene phone calls to the travel agent in Bali simply told us that the tickets were definitely confirmed, and that's all there was to it. The ticket office told us that they definitely weren't, and that's all there was to it.

"What about another flight?" we asked. Maybe, they said. Maybe in a week or two.

"A week or two?" exclaimed Gaynor, who had a proper job at the BBC to get back to.

"Moment," said one of the men, took our tickets and went away with them. About ten minutes later he returned and gave them to a second man who said, "Moment," and went away with them in turn. He returned fifteen minutes later, looked at us, and said, "Yes? What do you want to know?" We explained the situation all over again, whereupon he nodded, said, "Moment," and disappeared again. When, after a longish while had passed, we asked where he was, we were told that he had gone to visit his mother in Jakarta because he hadn't seen her in three years.

Had he taken our tickets with him? we enquired.

No, they were here somewhere, we were told. Did we want them?

Yes, we did, we explained. We were trying to get to La-buan Bajo.

This news seemed to cause considerable consternation, and within minutes everyone in the office had gone to lunch.

It became clear that the plane was going to leave without us. We had the option of doing the first part of the flight, as far as Bima and then being stranded there, but decided instead to stay in Bali and go and deal with the travel agent. No more Mr. Serene Guys.

A minibus took us back to the travel agency, where we stormed slowly up the stairs with all our baggage and angrily refused to sit and have coffee and listen to a machine which played "Greensleeves" whenever the phone ran. There was a sense of muted horror in the air as if one of us had died, but no one actually paid any attention to us for nearly an hour, so in the end we started to get angry again and were immediately shown into the office of the director of the agency, who sat us down and told us that the Indonesians were a proud race and that furthermore it was all the fault of the airline.

He then soothed at us a great deal, told us that he was a very powerful man in Bali, and explained that it did not help the situation that we got angry about it.

This was a point of view with which I had some natural sympathy, being something of a smiler and nodder myself, who generally registers anger and frustration by frowning a lot and going to sleep.

On the other hand, I couldn't help noticing that all the time we had merely smiled and nodded and laughed pleasantly when we had been laughed pleasantly at, nothing had happened and people had merely said "Moment, moment" a lot and gone to Jakarta or peered at us impassively through narrow wreaths of smoke. As soon as we had geared ourselves up to get angry and stamp our feet a bit, we had been instantly whisked to the office of the director of the travel agency, who was busy telling us that there was no point in us getting angry, and that he would arrange an extra flight specially for us to Labuan Bajo.

He tried to demonstrate the uselessness of stamping our feet to us with maps. "In these areas," he said, pointing to a

large wall map of half of Asia, "it works. East of this line here it doesn't work."

He explained that if you are traveling in Indonesia, you should allow four or five days for anything urgent to happen. As far as our missing plane seats were concerned, he said that this sort of thing happened all the time. Often some government official or other important person would decide that he needed a seat, and, of course, someone else would then lose theirs. We asked if this was what had happened to us. He said, no, it wasn't the reason, but it was the sort of reason we should bear in mind when thinking about these problems.

At this point we agreed to have the coffee.

He organised hotel rooms for us for the night, and a minibus tour of the island for the afternoon.

There is a good living to be made in Bali, we discovered, from pointing at animals. First find your animal, and then point at it.

If you set yourself up properly, you can even make a living from pointing at the person who is pointing at the animal. We found a very good example of this enterprise on the beach near the famous temple of Tanah Lot, and apparently it was a long-established and thriving business. Up on the beach there was a very low, wide cave, inside which, in a small cranny in the wall, a couple of yellow snakes had made their home.

Outside on the beach was a man who sat on a box and collected the money, and pointed at the man in the cave. Once you had paid your money, you crept into the cave, and the man in the cave pointed at the snakes.

Apart from this highlight, the guided tour was profoundly depressing. When we told our guide that we didn't want to go to all the tourist places, he took us instead to the places where they take tourists who say that they don't want to go to tourist places. These places are, of course, full of tourists. Which is not to say that we weren't tourists every bit as much

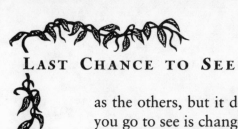

as the others, but it does highlight the irony that everything you go to see is changed by the very action of going to see it, which is the sort of problem which physicists have been wrestling with for most of this century. I'm not going to bang on about Bali being turned into a Bali Theme Park, in which Bali itself is gradually destroyed to make way for a tatty artificial version of what used to be there, because it is too familiar a process to come as news to anybody. I just want to let out a squeak of frustrated rage. I'm afraid I couldn't wait to leave the most beautiful place on earth.

The following day we finally succeeded in leaving Denpasar airport for Bima. Everyone knew us from the ructions of the day before, and this time the narrow man who had peered at us through wreaths of smoke was wreathed in smiles and terribly helpful.

This, though, was only softening us up.

At Bima we were told that there was no flight at all to Labuan Bajo till the following morning. Perhaps we would like to come back then? At that point we started to get into a bit of a frenzy, and then suddenly we were unexpectedly seized and pushed through the crowds and shoved on to a dilapidated little plane that was sitting fully loaded on the tarmac, waiting to take off for Labuan Bajo.

On the way to the plane, we couldn't help noticing that we passed our pile of intrepid baggage sitting on a small unregarded baggage cart out in the middle of the tarmac. Once we were on the plane, we sat and debated nervously with each other about whether we thought they might be thinking of loading it.

Eventually my nerve broke and I got off the plane and started running back across the tarmac. I was quickly intercepted by airline staff who demanded to know what I thought I was doing. I said "Baggage" a lot and pointed. They insisted that everything was okay, there was no problem, and that everything was under control. I persuaded them at last to come with me to the baggage cart standing in

the middle of the tarmac. With hardly a change of beat, they moved smoothly from assuring me that all our luggage was on board the plane to helping me actually get it on board.

That done, we could finally relax about the baggage and start seriously to worry about the state of the plane, which was terrifying.

The door to the cockpit remained open for the duration of the flight and might actually have been missing entirely. Mark told me that Air Merpati bought their planes second-hand from Air Uganda, but I think he was joking.

I have a cheerfully reckless view of this kind of air travel. It rarely bothers me at all. I don't think this is bravery, because I am frequently scared stiff in cars, particularly if I'm driving. But once you're in an airplane, everything is completely out of your hands, so you may as well just sit back and grin manically about the grinding and rattling noises the old wreck of a plane makes as the turbulence throws it around the sky. There's nothing you can do.

Mark was watching the instruments in the cockpit with curious intensity, and after a while said that half of them simply weren't working. I laughed, a little hectically, I admit, and said that it was probably just as well. If the instruments were working, they would probably distract and worry the pilots, and I'd rather they just got on with what they were doing. Mark thought that this was not at all an amusing observation, and he was clearly right, but nevertheless I laughed again, really rather a lot, and carried on laughing wildly for most of the rest of the flight. Mark turned and asked a passenger behind us if these planes ever crashed. Oh yes, he was told, but not to worry—there hadn't been a serious crash now in months.

Landing at Labuan Bajo was interesting, because the pilots couldn't get the flaps down. We were quite interested to know, for instance, as the trees at the end of the runway loomed closer and closer, and the two pilots were tugging with all their combined weight on the ceiling-mounted lever,

whether we were all going to live or not. At the last moment the lever suddenly gave way and we banged down onto the runway in a subdued and reflective frame of mind.

We climbed off the plane and after lengthy negotiations persuaded the airline staff to take our baggage off as well, since we thought we'd probably like to have it with us.

Two people met us at the airport "terminal," or hut. Their names were Kiri and Moose, and, like most Indonesians we met, they were small, willowy-slim, and healthy looking, and we had no idea who they were.

Kiri was a charming man with a squarish face, a shock of wavy black hair, and a thick black moustache that sat on his lip like a bar of chocolate. He had a voice that was very deep, but also very thin, with no substance behind it at all, so that he spoke in a sort of supercool croak. Most of the remarks he made consisted of a slow, lazy, streetwise smile and a couple of strangled rattles from the back of his throat. He always seemed to have something other on his mind. If he smiled at you, the smile never settled on you but ended up somewhere in the middle distance. Moose was much more straightforward, though it quickly turned out that Moose was not "Moose" but "Mus" and was short for Hieronymus. I felt a little stupid for having heard it as "Moose." It was unlikely that an Indonesian islander would be named after a large Canadian deer. Almost as unlikely, I suppose, as him being called Hieronymus with a silent "Hierony."

The person we had been expecting was a Mr. Condo (pronounced *Chondo*), who was to be our guide. I was puzzled as to why he alone among all the Indonesians we had met so far was called "Mr." It lent him an air of mystery and glamour which he wasn't there to dispel because he had, apparently, gone diving. He would, Kiri and Moose explained to us, be along shortly, and they had come along to tell us that.

We thanked them, loaded all of our baggage into the back of their pickup truck, and sat on top of it as we bumped

away from the arrivals hut toward the town of Labuan Bajo. We had been told by someone on the plane that there were only three trucks on the whole of the island of Flores, and we passed six of them on the way in. Virtually everything we were told in Indonesia turned out not to be true, sometimes almost immediately. The only exception to this was when we were told that something would happen immediately, in which case it turned out not to be true over an extended period of time.

Because of our experiences of the day before, we made a point of stopping at the Merpati Airlines hut on the way and reconfirming our seats on the return flight. The office was manned by a man with flip-flops and a field radio, with which he made all the flight arrangements. He didn't have a pen, so he simply had to remember them as best he could. He said he wished we had bought single tickets rather than returns, so that we could have bought our return tickets from them. No one, he said, ever bought tickets from them and they could use the money.

We asked him how many people were on the flight back. He looked at a list and said eight. I noticed, looking over his shoulder, that there was only one person on the list other than the three of us, and I asked him how he had arrived at the figure of eight. That was simple, he explained. There were always eight people on the flight.

As it turned out, a few days later, he was exactly right. There may be some principle lying hidden in this fact which British Airways and TWA and Lufthansa, etc., could profit from enormously, if only they could work out what it is.

The road into town was dusty. The air was far hotter and more humid than in Bali, and thick with the heady smells from the trees and shrubs. I asked Mark if he recognised the smells of any of the trees, and he said that he didn't, he was a zoologist. He thought he could detect the smell of sulphur-crested cockatoos in amongst it all, but that was all he would commit himself to.

Soon these minor evanescent odours were replaced by the magisterial pong of Labuan Bajo's drains. The truck, as we clattered into town, was surrounded by scampering, smiling children, who were delighted to see us, and keen to show off a new thing they had found to play with, which was a chicken with only one leg. The long main street was lined with several more of Flores's three trucks, noisy with the sounds of the children and the scratchy gargling of the tape-recorded muezzin blaring from the minaret which was perched precariously on top of the corrugated iron mosque. The gutters seemed inexplicably to be full of cheerfully bright green slime.

A guest house or small hotel in Indonesia is called a *losmen,* and we went to wait in the main one in town for Mr. Condo to turn up. We didn't check in because we were meant to be setting off for Komodo directly that afternoon, and anyway, the losmen was practically empty, so there didn't seem to be any urgency. Mark, Gaynor, and I whiled away the time in the covered courtyard which served as a dining room, drinking a few beers and chatting to the odd extra guests who arrived from time to time. By the time we finally twigged, as the afternoon wore on with no Mr. Condo, that we were not going to be getting to Komodo that day after all, the losmen had filled up nicely and there was a sudden panic about getting ourselves somewhere to sleep.

A small boy came out and said they still had a bedroom if we would like it, and took us up some rickety steps. The corridor we walked along to get to the bedroom turned out itself to be the bedroom. We were misled by the fact that it didn't have any beds in it, but we agreed that it would be fine and returned to the courtyard, to be greeted at last by Mr. Condo, a small charismatic man, who said that everything was organised and we would be leaving for Komodo in a boat at seven in the morning.

What about the goat? we asked anxiously.

He shrugged. What goat? he asked.

Won't we need a goat?

There were plenty of goats on Komodo, he assured us. Unless we wanted one for the voyage?

We said that we didn't feel that we particularly did, and he said that he only mentioned it as it seemed to be the only thing we weren't intending to take with us. We took this to be a satirical reference to the pile of intrepid baggage with which we were surrounded and laughed politely, so he wished us good night and told us to get some good sleep.

Sleeping in Labuan Bajo, however, is something of an endurance test.

Being woken at dawn by the cockerels is not in itself a problem. The problem arises when the cockerels get confused as to when dawn actually is. They suddenly explode into life, squawking and screaming at about one o'clock in the morning. At about one-thirty they eventually realise their mistake and shut up, just as the major dogfights of the evening are getting under way. These usually start with a few minor bouts between the more enthusiastic youngsters, and then the full chorus of heavyweights weighs in with a fine impression of what it might be like to fall into the pit of hell with the London Symphony Orchestra.

It is then quite an education to learn that two cats fighting can make easily as much noise as forty dogs. It is a pity to have to learn this at two-fifteen in the morning, but then the cats have a lot to complain about in Labuan Bajo. They all have their tails docked at birth, which is supposed to bring good luck, though presumably not to the cats.

Once the cats have concluded their reflections on this, the cockerels suddenly get the idea that it's dawn again and let rip. It isn't, of course. Dawn is still two hours away, and you still have the delivery-van horn-blowing competition to get through to the accompaniment of the major divorce proceedings that have suddenly erupted in the room next door.

27
▼▼▼

At last things calm down and your eyelids begin to slide thankfully together in the blessed predawn hush, and then, about five minutes later, the cockerels finally get it right.

An hour or two later, bleary and rattled, we stood on the waterfront surrounded by our piles of expeditionary baggage and gazed as intrepidly as we could across twenty miles of the roughest, most turbulent seas in the East—the wild and dangerous meeting point of two immense opposing bodies of water, a roiling turmoil of vortices and riptides.

It was like a millpond.

Ripples from distant fishing boats spread out across the wide sea toward the shore. The early sun shone across it like a sheet. Lesser frigate birds and white-bellied sea eagles wheeled serenely above us, according to Mark. They looked like black specks to me.

We were there but Mr. Condo was not. After about an hour, however, Kiri turned up to fulfill his regular role of explaining that Mr. Condo was not coming, but that he, Kiri, was coming instead, and so was his guitar. And the captain wasn't the actual captain, but was the captain's father. And we were going in a different boat. The good news was that it was definitely Komodo we would be going to and the trip should only take about four hours.

The boat was quite a smart twenty-three-foot fishing vessel called the *Raodah,* and the entire complement, once we were all loaded and under way, consisted of the three of us, Kiri, the captain's father, two small boys aged about twelve who ran the boat, and four chickens.

The day was calm and delightful. The two boys scampered about the boat like cats, rapidly unfurling and raising the sails whenever there was a whisper of wind, then lowering them again, starting the engine, and falling asleep whenever the wind died. For once there was nothing we had to do and nothing we could do, so we lounged around on the deck watching the sea go by, watching the crested terns and sea

eagles that flew over us, and watching the flying fish that swarmed occasionally around the boat.

The four chickens sat in the boat's prow and watched us.

One of the more disturbing aspects of travel in remote areas is the necessity of taking your food with you in nonperishable form. For Westerners who are used to getting their chickens wrapped in polythene from the supermarket, it is an uncomfortable experience to share a long ride on a small boat with four live chickens who are eyeing you with a deep and dreadful suspicion which you are in no position to allay.

Despite the fact that an Indonesian island chicken has probably had a much more natural and pleasant life than one raised on a battery farm in England, people who wouldn't think twice about buying something oven-ready become much more upset about a chicken that they've been on a boat with, so there is probably buried in the Western psyche a deep taboo about eating anything you've been introduced to socially.

As it happened, we would not be eating all four of them ourselves. Whichever god it is in the complicated Hindu pantheon who has the lowly task of determining the fate of chickens was obviously in a rumbustious mood that day and was planning a little havoc of his own.

And then at last the island of Komodo was ahead of us, creeping slowly toward us from the horizon. The colour of the sea around the boat was changing from the heavy, inky black it had been for the last few hours to a much lighter, translucent blue, but the island itself seemed, perhaps to our impressionable senses, to be a dark and sombre mass looming over the water.

As it approached, its gloomy form gradually resolved into great serrated heaps of rocks and, behind them, heavy undulating hills. Closer still we could begin to make out the details of the vegetation. There were palm trees, but in meager numbers. They were stuck sporadically across the brows of the hills, as if the island had spines, or as if someone had chucked

29
▼▼▼

little darts into the hills. It reminded me of the illustration from *Gulliver's Travels,* in which Gulliver has been tethered to the ground by the Lilliputians, and has dozens of tiny Lilliputian spears sticking into him.

The images that the island presented to the imagination were very hard to avoid. The rocky outcrops took on the shape of massive triangular teeth, and the dark and moody grey-brown hills undulated like the heavy folds of a lizard's skin. I knew that if I were a mariner in unknown waters, the first thing I would write on my charts at this moment would be "Here be dragons."

But the harder I looked at the island as it crept past our starboard bow, and the harder I tried to filter out the promptings of a suggestible imagination, the more the images nevertheless insisted themselves upon me. The ridge of a hill that stretched in a thick folding shape down into the water, heavily wrinkled around its folds, had the contours of a lizard's legs—not in actual shape, of course, but in the natural interplay of its contours, and in the heavy thickness of its textures.

30
▼▼▼

This was the first time that I had such an impression, but several times during the subsequent trips that we made during this year the same feeling crept up on me: each new type of terrain we encountered in different parts of the world would seem to have a particular palette of colours, textures, shapes, and contours that made it characteristically itself, and the forms of life that you would find in that terrain would often seem to be drawn from that same distinctive palette. There are obvious mechanisms we know about to account for some of this, of course: for many creatures, camouflage is a survival mechanism, and evolution will select in its favour. But the scale on which these intuited, perhaps half-imagined, correspondences seem to occur is much larger and more general than that.

We are currently beginning to arrive at a lot of new ideas about the way that shapes emerge in nature, and it is not

impossible to imagine that as we discover more about fractal geometry, the "strange attractors" that lie at the heart of newly emerging theories of chaos, and the way in which the mathematics of growth and erosion interact, we may discover that these apparent echoes of shape and texture are not entirely fanciful or coincidental. Maybe.

I suggested something along these lines to Mark and he said I was being absurd. Since he was looking at exactly the same landscape as I was, I have to allow that it might all simply have been my imagination, half-baked as it was in the Indonesian sun.

We moored at a long, rickety, wooden jetty that stuck out from the middle of a wide pale beach. At the landward end the jetty was surmounted by an archway, nailed to the top of which was a wooden board which welcomed us to Komodo, and therefore served slightly to diminish our sense of intrepidness.

The moment we passed under the archway there was suddenly a strong smell. You had to go through it to get the smell. Until you'd been through the archway you hadn't arrived and you didn't get the strong, thick, musty, smell of Komodo.

The next blow to our sense of intrepidness was the rather neatly laid-out path. This led from the end of the jetty parallel to the shore toward the next and major blow to our sense of intrepidness, which was a visitors' village.

This was a group of fairly ramshackle wooden buildings: an administration centre from which the island (which is a wildlife reserve) is run, a cafeteria terrace, and a small museum. Behind these, ranged around the inside of a steep semicircular slope, were about half a dozen visitors' huts—on stilts.

It was about lunchtime, and there were nearly a dozen people sitting in the cafeteria eating noodles and drinking 7-Up; Americans, Dutch, you name it. Where had they come from? How had they got here? What was going on?

Outside the administration hut was a wooden sign with regulations all over it, such as "Report to National Park office," "Travel outside visitors' center only with guards," "Wear pants and shoes," and "Watch for snakes."

Lying on the ground underneath this was a small stuffed dragon. I say small because it was only about four feet long. It had been modeled in completely spread-eagled posture, lying flat on the ground with its forelimbs stretched out in front and its back limbs lying alongside its long tapering tail. I was a little startled to see it for a moment, but then went up to have a look at it.

It opened its eyes and had a look at me.

I rocketed backward with a yell of astonishment, which provoked barks of derisive laughter from the terrace.

"It's just a dragon!" called out an American girl.

I went over.

"Have you all been here long?" I asked.

"Oh, hours," she said. "We came over on the ferry from Labuan Bajo. Done the dragons. Bored with them. The food's terrible."

"What ferry?" I asked.

"Comes over most days."

"Oh. Oh, I see. From Labuan Bajo?"

"You have to go and sign the visitors' book in the office," she said, pointing at it.

Rather ruffled, I went and joined Mark and Gaynor.

"This isn't at all what I expected," said Mark, standing there in the middle of our pile of intrepid baggage, holding the four chickens. "Did we need to bring these?" he asked Kiri.

Kiri said that it was always a good idea to bring chickens for the kitchen. Otherwise we'd just have to eat fish and noodles.

"I think I prefer fish," said Gaynor.

Kiri explained that she was wrong and that she preferred chicken to fish. Westerners, he explained, preferred chicken.

It was well known. Fish was only cheap food for peasants. We would be eating chicken, which was sexy and which we preferred.

He took the chickens, which were tethered together with a long piece of string, put them down by our baggage, and ushered us up the steps to the park office, where one of the park guards gave us forms and a pencil. Just as we were starting to fill them in, giving details of our passport numbers, date, country, and town of birth, and so on, there was a sudden commotion outside.

At first we paid it no mind, wrestling as we were to remember our mothers' maiden names, and trying to work out who to elect as next of kin, but the racket outside increased, and we suddenly realised that it was the sound of distressed chickens. Our chickens.

We rushed outside. The stuffed dragon was attacking our chickens. It had one of them in its mouth and was shaking it, but as soon as it saw us and others closing in, it scurried rapidly around the corner of the building and off across the clearing behind in a cloud of dust, dragging the other distraught chickens tumbling along in the dust behind it, still tethered together with the string and screeching.

After the dragon put about thirty yards between it and us, it paused, and with a vicious jerk of its head bit through the string, releasing the other three chickens, which scrambled off toward the trees, shrieking and screaming and running in ever-decreasing circles as park guards careered after them trying to round them up. The dragon relieved of its excess chickens, galloped off into thick undergrowth.

With a lot of "After you," "No, after you," we ran carefully toward where it had disappeared and arrived breathless and a little nervous. We peered in.

The undergrowth covered a large bank, and the dragon had crawled up the bank and stopped. The thick vegetation prevented us from getting closer than a yard to the thing, but then, we weren't trying terribly hard.

33
▼▼▼

It lay there quite still. Protruding from between its jaws was the back end of the chicken, its scrawny legs quietly working the air. The dragon lizard watched us unconcernedly with the one eye that was turned toward us, a round, dark brown eye.

There is something profoundly disturbing about watching an eye that is watching you, particularly when the eye that is watching you is almost the same size as your eye, and the thing it is watching you out of is a lizard. The lizard's blink was also disturbing. It wasn't the normal rapid reflex movement that you expect from a lizard, but a slow, considered blink which made you feel that it was thinking about what it was doing.

The back end of the chicken struggled feebly for a moment, and the dragon chomped its jaw a little to let the chicken's struggles push it farther down its throat. This happened a couple more times, until there was only one scrawny chicken foot still sticking ridiculously out of the creature's mouth. Otherwise it did not move. It simply watched us. In the end it was us who slunk away trembling with an inexplicable cold horror.

34
▼▼▼

Why? we wondered as we sat in the terrace cafeteria and tried to calm ourselves with 7-Up. The three of us were sitting ashen-faced as if we had just witnessed a foul and malignant murder. At least if we had been watching a murder, the murderer wouldn't have been looking us impassively in the eye as he did it. Maybe it was the feeling of cold, unflinching arrogance that so disturbed us. But whatever malign emotions we tried to pin on to the lizard, we knew that they weren't the lizards emotions at all, only ours. The lizard was simply going about its lizardly business in a simple, straightforward lizardly way. It didn't know anything about the horror, the guilt, the shame, the ugliness that we, uniquely guilty and ashamed animals, were trying to foist on it. So we got it all straight back at us, as if reflected in the mirror of its single unwavering and disinterested eye.

Subdued with the thought that we had somehow been hor-
rified by our own reflection, we sat quietly and waited for
lunch.

Lunch.

In view of all the events of the day so far, lunch suddenly
seemed to be a very complicated thing to contemplate.

Lunch, as it turned out, was not a chicken. It wasn't a
chicken because the dragon had eaten it. How the kitchen
was able to determine that the chicken the dragon had eaten
was the precise one that they were otherwise going to do for
lunch was not clear to us, but apparently that was the reason
we were having plain noodles, and we were grateful for it.

We talked about how easy it was to make the mistake of
anthropomorphising animals, and projecting our own feelings and perceptions on to them, where they were inappro-
priate and didn't fit. We simply had no idea what it was *like*
being an extremely large lizard, and neither, for that matter,
did the lizard, because it was not self-conscious about being
an extremely large lizard, it just got on with the business of
being one. To react with revulsion to its behaviour was to
make the mistake of applying criteria that are only appropriate to the business of being human. We each make our own
accommodation with the world and learn to survive in it in
different ways. What works as successful behaviour for us
does not work for lizards, and vice versa.

"For instance," said Mark, "we don't eat our own babies
if they happen to be within reach when we're feeling a little
peckish."

"What?" said Gaynor, putting down her knife and fork.

"A baby dragon is just food as far as an adult is concerned," Mark continued. "It moves about and has got a bit
of meat on it. It's food. If they ate them all, of course, the
species would die out, so that wouldn't work very well. Most
animals survive because the adults have acquired an instinct
not to eat their babies. The dragons survive because the baby
dragons have acquired an instinct to climb trees. The adults

35
▼▼▼

are too big to do it, so the babies just sit up in trees till they're big enough to look after themselves. Some babies get caught though, which works fine. It sees them through times when food is scarce and helps to keep the population within sustainable levels. Sometimes they just eat them because they're there."

"How many of these things are there left?" I asked quietly.

"About five thousand."

"And how many did there used to be?"

"About five thousand. As far as anyone can tell, that's roughly how many there have always been."

"So they're not particularly endangered?"

"Well, they are, because only three hundred and fifty of them are breeding females. We don't know if that's a typical number or not, but it seems pretty low. Furthermore, if an animal has a low population and lives in a very restricted area, like just a few small islands in the case of the dragons, it's particularly vulnerable to changes in its habitat, and wherever human beings arrive, habitats start changing pretty quickly."

"So we shouldn't be here."

"It's arguable," said Mark. "If no one was here taking an interest, the chances are very strong that something could go wrong. Just one forest fire, or a disease in the deer population, could wipe out dragons. And there's also the worry that the growing human population on the islands would start to feel that they could very well live without them. They are very dangerous animals. There's not merely the danger of being eaten by one. If you just get bitten, you are in very serious trouble. You see, when a dragon attacks a horse or a buffalo, it doesn't necessarily expect to kill it there and then. If it gets involved in a fight, it might get injured, and there's no benefit in that, so sometimes the dragon will just bite it and walk away. But the bacteria that live in a dragon's saliva are so virulent that the wounds will not heal and the animal

will usually die in a few days of septicemia, whereupon the dragon can eat it at leisure. Or another dragon can eat it if it happens to find it first—they're not really fussed. It's good for the species that there is a regular supply of badly injured and dying animals about the place.

"There was a well-known case of a Frenchman who was bitten by a dragon and eventually died in Paris two years later. The wound festered and would just never heal. Unfortunately, there were no dragons in Paris to take advantage of it, so the strategy broke down on that occasion, but generally it works well. The point is that these things are buggers to have living on your doorstep, and though the villagers on Komodo and Rinca have been pretty tolerant, there has been a history of attacks and deaths, and it's possible that as the human population grows, there will be a greater conflict of interest and rather less patience with the idea of not being able to go off for a wander without running the risk of having your leg bitten off and your entrails ripped out by a passing dragon.

"So, as we've discovered, Komodo is now a protected national park. We've got to the point where it takes active and deliberate intervention to save rare species, and that's usually sustained by public interest. And public interest is sustained by public access. If it's carefully controlled and disruption is kept to a minimum, then it works well and is fine. I *think*. I won't pretend that I don't feel uneasy about it."

"I feel very uneasy about the whole place," said Gaynor with a shudder. "There's a kind of creeping malignancy about it."

"Just your imagination," said Mark. "For a naturalist, it's paradise."

There was suddenly a slithering noise on the roof of the terrace, and a large snake fell past us to the ground. Instantly a couple of park guards rushed out and chased the thing off into the bush.

"That wasn't my imagination," said Gaynor.

"I know," said Mark enthusiastically. "This is wonderful."

In the afternoon, accompanied by Kiri and a guard, we went off to explore. We found no dragons, but as we thrashed recklessly through the undergrowth, we encountered instead a bird, and it was one that I felt very much at home with.

I have a well-deserved reputation for being something of a gadget freak, and am rarely happier than when spending an entire day programming my computer to perform automatically a task that it would otherwise take me a good ten seconds to do by hand. Ten seconds, I tell myself, is ten seconds. Time is valuable and ten seconds' worth of it is well worth the investment of a day's happy activity working out a way of saving it.

The bird we came across was called a megapode, and it has a very similar outlook on life.

38
▼▼▼

It looks a little like a lean, sprightly chicken, though it has the advantage over chickens that it can fly, if a little heavily, and is therefore better able to escape from dragons, which can only fly in fairy tales, and in some of the nightmares with which I was plagued while trying to sleep on Komodo.

The important thing is that the megapode has worked out a wonderful labour-saving device for itself. The labour it wishes to save is the time-consuming activity of sitting on its nest all day incubating its eggs, when it could be out and about doing things.

I have to say at this point that we didn't actually come across the bird itself, though we thought we glimpsed one scuttling through the undergrowth. We did, however, come across its labour-saving device, which is something that it's hard to miss. It was a conical mound of thickly packed earth and rotting vegetation, about six feet high and six feet wide at its base. In fact, it was considerably higher than it appeared because the mound would have been built on a hol-

low in the ground, which itself would have been about three feet deep.

I've just spent a cheerful hour of my time writing a program on my computer that will tell me instantly what the volume of the mound was. It's a very neat and sexy program with all sorts of pop-up menus and things, and the advantage of doing it the way I have is that on any future occasion on which I need to know the volume of a megapode nest, given its basic dimensions, my computer will give the answer in less than a second, which is a wonderful saving of time. The downside, I suppose, is that I cannot conceive of any future occasion that I am likely to need to know the volume of a megapode nest, but no matter: the volume of this mound is a little over nine cubic yards.

What the mound is is an automatic incubator. The heat generated by the chemical reactions of the rotting vegetation keeps the eggs that are buried deep inside it warm—and not merely warm. By judicious additions or subtractions of material from the mound, the megapode is able to keep it at the precise temperature that the eggs require in order to incubate properly.

So all the megapode has to do to incubate its eggs is merely to dig three cubic yards of earth out of the ground, fill it with three cubic yards of rotting vegetation, collect a further six cubic yards of vegetation, build it into a mound, and then continually monitor the heat it is producing and run about adding bits or taking bits away.

And thus it saves itself all the bother of sitting on its eggs from time to time.

This cheered me up immensely, and the good mood it put me into lasted all the way back to the visitors' village and up to the precise point when we walked in through the door of the hut that we had been assigned as sleeping quarters.

It was quite large and constructed, as I have said, on stilts —for obvious reasons. However, the wood of which it was built was half rotten, there were damp and stinking mat-

tresses in the small bedrooms, ominously large spiders' webs in all the corners, dead rats on the floor, and the stench of an overflowing lavatory.

We tried gamely to sleep there that night, but in the end were driven out by the sheer noise of the rats fighting the snakes in the roof cavity, and eventually we took our sleeping bags down to the boat and slept on its deck.

We awoke early, cold and damp with the dew, but feeling safe. We rolled up our bags and made our way back along the rickety jetty and under the arch. Once again, as soon as we had passed through the arch, the smell of the place assailed us and we were in that malign other world, Komodo.

This morning, we had been told, we would definitely see dragons. Big dragons. We didn't know precisely what it was we were in for, but clearly it was not what we had originally expected. It didn't look as if we would be pegging a dead goat out on the ground and then hiding up a tree all day.

The day was to consist almost entirely of things we had not been expecting, starting with the arrival of a group of about two dozen American tourists on a specially chartered boat. They were mostly of early retirement age, festooned with cameras, polyester leisure suits, gold-rimmed glasses and Midwestern accents, and I didn't think that they would all be sitting up a tree all day either.

We were severely put out by their arrival and felt that the last vestige of any sense of intrepidness we were still trying to hold on to was finally slipping away.

We found a guard and asked what was going on. He said we could go on ahead now if we wanted to avoid the large party, so we set off with him immediately. We had a walk of about three or four miles through the forest along a path that was obviously well prepared and well trodden. The air was hot and dusty, and we walked with a sense of queasy uncertainty about how the day was going to go. After a while we became aware of the faint sound of a bell moving along ahead of us, and quickened our footsteps to find out what it was. We rounded a corner, and were confronted with some stomach-turning reality.

Up till now there had been something dreamlike about the whole experience. It was as if the action of walking through the archway and ingesting the musty odor of the island spirited you into an illusory world, in which words like *dragon* and *snake* and *goat* acquired fantastical meanings that had no analogue in the real world, and no consequence in it either. Now I had the feeling that the dream was slithering down the slope into nightmare, and that it was the sort of nightmare from which you would wake to discover that you had indeed wet the bed, that someone was indeed shaking you and shouting, and that the acrid smell of smoke was indeed your house incinerating itself.

Ahead of us on the path was a young goat. It had a bell and a rope around its neck and was being led unwillingly along the pathway by another guard. We followed it numbly. Occasionally it would trot along hesitantly for a few paces, and then an appalling dread would seem suddenly to seize it and it would push its forelegs into the ground, put its head down, and struggle desperately against the tugging of the rope, bleating and crying. The guard would pull roughly on the rope and swipe at the goat's hindquarters with a bunch of leafy twigs he was carrying in his other hand, and the goat would at last tumble forward and trot along a few more paces, light-headed with fear. There was nothing for the goat to see to make it so afraid, and nothing, so far as we could tell, to hear; but who knows what the goat could smell in that place toward which we all were moving.

Our deeply sinking spirits were next clouded sideways from a totally unexpected direction. We came across a circle of concrete set in the middle of a clearing. The circle was about twenty feet across, and had two parallel black stripes painted on it, with another black stripe at right angles to them, connecting their centres. It took us a few moments to work out what the symbol was and what it meant. Then we got it. It was just an "H." The circle was a helicopter pad. Whatever it was that was going to happen to this goat was something people came by helicopter to see.

We trotted on, numb and light-headed, suddenly finding meaningless things to laugh wildly and hysterically at, as if we were walking willfully toward something that would destroy us as well.

Leading from the helipad was a yet more formal pathway. It was a couple of yards wide with a stout wooden fence about two feet high along either side. We followed this along for a couple of hundred yards until we came at last to a wide gully, about ten feet deep, and here there were a number of things to see.

To our left was a kind of bandstand. Several rows of bench seats were banked up behind one another, with a sloping wooden roof to protect them from the sun and other inclemencies in the weather. Tied to the front rail of the bandstand were both ends of a long piece of blue nylon rope, which ran out and down into the gully, where it was slung over a pulley wheel which hung from the branches of a small bent tree. A small iron hook hung from the rope.

Stationed around the tree, basking in the dull light of a hot but overcast day, and in the stench of rotten death, were six large, muddy grey dragon lizards.

The largest of them was probably about ten feet long.

It was at first quite difficult to gauge their size. We were not that close as yet, the light was too blear and grey to model them clearly to the eye, and the eye was simply not accustomed to equating something with the shape of a lizard with something of that size.

I stared at them awhile, aghast, until I realised that Mark was tapping me on the arm. I turned to look. On the other side of the short fence, a large dragon was approaching us.

It had emerged from the undergrowth, attracted, no doubt, by the knowledge that the arrival of human beings meant that it was feeding time. We learned later that the group of dragons that hang out in the gully rarely go very far from it and now do very little at all other than lie and wait to be fed.

The dragon lizard padded toward us, slapping its feet down aggressively, first its front left and back right, then vice versa, carrying its great weight easily and springily, with the swinging, purposeful gait of a bully. Its long, narrow, pale, forked tongue flickered in and out, testing the air for the smell of dead things.

It reached the far side of the fence, and then began to range back and forth tetchily, waiting for action, swinging and scraping its heavy tail across the dusty earth. Its rough, scaly skin hung a little loosely over its body, like chain mail, gathering to a series of cowl-like folds just behind its long death's head of a face. Its legs are thick and muscular, and end in claws such as you'd expect to find at the bottom of a brass table leg.

The thing is just a monitor lizard, and yet it is massive to a degree that is unreal. As it rears its head up over the fence and around as it turns, you wonder how it's done, what trickery is involved.

At that moment the party of tourists began to straggle toward us along the path, cheery and unimpressed, wanting to know what was up, what was happening. Look, there's one of those dragons! Ooh, it's a big one. Nasty-looking feller!

And now the worst of it was about to happen.

At a discreet distance behind the bandstand, the goat was being slaughtered. Two park guards held the struggling, bleating creature down on the ground with its neck across a log and hacked its head off with a machete, holding the bunch of leafy twigs against it to staunch the eruption of blood. The goat took several minutes to die.

Once it was dead, they cut off one of its back legs for the dragon behind the fence, then took the rest of the body and fastened it on to the hook on the blue nylon rope. It rocked

43
▼▼▼

and swayed in the breeze as they winched it down to the dragons lying in the gully.

The dragons took only a lethargic interest in it for a while. They were very well-fed and sleepy dragons. At last one reared itself up, approached the hanging carcass, and ripped slowly at its soft underbelly. A great muddle of intestines slipped out of the goat and flopped over the dragon's head. They lay there for a while, steaming gently. The dragon seemed, for the moment, not to take any further interest.

Another dragon then heaved itself into motion and approached. It sniffed and licked at the air, and then started to eat the intestines of the goat from off the head of the first dragon, until the first dragon rounded on it and started to claim part of its meal for itself. At first nip, a thick green liquid flooded out of the glistening grey coils, and as the meal proceeded, the head of each dragon in turn became wet with the green liquid.

"Boy, this makes it big, Pauline," said a man standing near me, watching through his binoculars. "It makes it bigger than it is. You know, with these it's the size I really thought we'd be seeing." He handed the binoculars to his wife.

"Oh, that really does magnify it!" she said.

"It really is a superb pair of binoculars, Pauline. And they're not heavy either."

Others of the group clustered around.

"May I take a look? Whose are they?"

"My gosh, Howard would adore these!"

"Al? Al, take a look at these binoculars—and see how heavy they are!"

Just as I was making the charitable assumption that the binoculars were just a diversion from having actually to watch the hellish floor show in the pit, the woman who now had possession of them suddenly exclaimed delightedly, "Gulp, gulp gulp! All gone! What a digestive system! Now he's smelling us!"

"He probably wants fresher meat," growled her husband. "Live, on the hoof!"

It was in fact at least an hour or so before all of the goat was gone, by which time the party had drifted, chatting, back to the village. As they did so, a lone Englishwoman in the party confided to us that she didn't actually care much about the dragons. "I like the landscape," she said airily. "The dragons are just thrown in. And of course, with all the strings and the goats and the tourists, well, it's just comedy really. If you were walking by yourself and you came across one, that might be different, but it's kind of like a puppet show."

When the last of them had left, a park guard told us that if we wished to we could climb down into the gully and see the dragons close up, and with swimming heads we did so. Two guards came with us, armed with long sticks, which branched into a "Y" at the end. They used these to push the dragons' necks away when they came too close or began to look aggressive.

We clambered and slithered down the slope, almost too scared to know or care what we were doing, and within a few minutes I found myself standing just two feet from the largest of the dragons. It regarded me without much interest, having plenty already to feed on. A length of dripping intestine was hanging from its open jaws, and its face was glistening with blood and saliva. The inside of its mouth was a pale, hard pink, and its fetid breath, together with the hot foul air of the gully, produced a stench so overpowering that our eyes were stinging and streaming and we were half faint with nausea.

All that remained by now of the goat which we had followed as it struggled bleating down the pathway ahead of us was one bloody and dismembered leg hanging by its ankle from the hook on the blue nylon rope. One dragon alone was still interested in it, and was gnawing moodily at the thigh muscles. Then it got a proper grip on the whole leg and tried

45
▼▼▼

with vicious twists of its head to pull it off the hook, but the leg was held fast at the ankle bone. Then, astoundingly, the dragon began instead very slowly to swallow the leg whole. It pulled and tugged, and maneuvered itself, so that more and more of the leg was pushed down its throat, until all that protruded was the hoof and the hook. After a while the dragon gave up struggling with it and simply squatted there, frozen in this posture for at least ten minutes until at last a guard did it the favor of hacking the hook away with his machete. The very last piece of the goat slithered away into the lizard's maw, where bones, hooves, horns, and all would now slowly be dissolved by the corrosive power of the enzymes that live in a Komodo dragon's digestive system.

We made our excuses and left.

The first of our three remaining chickens made its appearance at lunch, but our mood wasn't right for it. We pushed the scrawny bits of it listlessly around our plates and could find little to say.

In the afternoon we took the boat to Komodo village, where we met a woman who was the only known survivor of a dragon attack. A giant lizard had gone for her while she was out working in the fields, and by the time her screams had brought her neighbours and their dogs to rescue her and beat the creature away, her leg was in tatters. Intensive surgery in Bali saved her from having it amputated and, miraculously, she fought off the infection and lived, though her leg was still a mangled ruin. On the neighbouring island of Rinca, we were told, a four-year-old boy had been snatched by a dragon as he lay playing on the steps of his home. The living build their houses on stilts, but on these islands not even the dead are safe, and they are buried with sharp rocks piled high on their graves.

For all my rational Western intellect and education, I was for the moment overwhelmed by a primitive sense of living in a world ordered by a malign and perverted god, and it

coloured my view of everything that afternoon—even the coconuts. The villagers sold us some and split them open for us. They are almost perfectly designed. You first make a hole and drink the milk, then you split open the nut with a machete and slice off a segment of the shell, which forms a perfect implement for scooping out the coconut flesh inside. What makes you wonder about the nature of this god character is that he creates something that is so perfectly designed to be of benefit to human beings and then hangs it twenty feet above their heads on a tree with no branches.

Here's a good trick, let's see how they cope with this. Oh, look! They've managed to find a way of climbing the tree. I didn't think they'd be able to do that. All right, let's see them get the thing open. Hmm, so they've found out how to temper steel now, have they? Okay, no more Mr. Nice Guy. Next time they go up that tree, I'll have a dragon waiting for them at the bottom.

I can only think that the business with the apple must have upset him more than I realised.

I went and sat on the beach by a mangrove tree and gazed out at the quiet ripples of the sea. Some fish were jumping up the beach and into the tree, which struck me as an odd thing for a fish to do, but I tried not to be judgmental about it. I was feeling pretty raw about my own species, and not much inclined to raise a quizzical eyebrow at others. The fish could play about in trees as much as they liked if it gave them pleasure, so long as they didn't try to justify themselves or tell one another it was a malign god who made them want to play in trees.

I was feeling pretty raw about my own species because we presume to draw a distinction between what we call good and what we call evil. We find our images of what we call evil in things outside ourselves, in creatures that know nothing of such matters, so that we can feel revolted by them, and, by contrast, good about ourselves. And if they won't be revolting enough of their own accord, we stoke them up with

a goat. They don't want the goat, they don't need it. If they wanted one, they'd find it themselves. The only truly revolting thing that happens to the goat is in fact done by us.

So why didn't we say something? Like "Don't kill the goat"?

Well, there are a number of possible reasons:

—If the goat hadn't been killed for us, it would have been killed for someone else—for the party of American tourists, for instance.
—We didn't really realise what was going to happen till it was too late to stop it.
—The goat didn't lead a particularly nice life, anyway. Particularly not today.
—Another dragon would probably have got it later.
—If it hadn't been the goat, the dragons would have got something else, like a deer or something.
—We were reporting the incident for this book and for the BBC. It was important that we went through the whole experience so that people would know about it in detail. That's well worth a goat.
—We felt too polite to say, "Please don't kill the goat on our account."
—We were a bunch of lily-livered rationalising turds.

The great thing about being the only species that makes a distinction between right and wrong is that we can make up the rules for ourselves as we go along.

The fish were still hopping harmlessly up and down the tree. They were about three inches long, brown and black, with little bobble eyes set very close together on the top of their heads. They hopped along using their fins as crutches.

"Mudskippers," said Mark, who happened along at that moment. He squatted down to look at them.

"What are they doing in the tree?" I asked.

"You could say they were experimenting," said Mark. "If they find they can make a better living on the land than in the water, then in the course of time and evolution they may come to stay on the land. They absorb a certain amount of oxygen through their skin at the moment, but they have to rush back into the sea from time to time for a mouthful of water, which they process through their gills. But that can change. It's happened before."

"What do you mean?"

"Well, it's probable that life on this planet started in the oceans, and that marine creatures migrated onto the land in search of new habitats. There's one fish that existed about three hundred and fifty million years ago that was very like a mudskipper. It came up on to the land using its fins as crutches. It's possible that it was the ancestor of all land-living vertebrates."

"Really? What was it called?"

"I don't think it had a name at the time."

"So this fish is what we were like three hundred and fifty million years ago?"

"Quite possibly."

"So in three hundred and fifty million years' time one of its descendants could be sitting on the beach here with a camera around its neck watching other fish hopping out of the sea?"

"No idea. That's for science-fiction novelists to think about. Zoologists can only say what we think has happened so far."

I suddenly felt, well, terribly *old* as I watched a mudskipper hopping along with what now seemed to me like a wonderful sense of hopeless, boundless naive optimism. It had such a terribly, terribly, terribly long way to go. I hoped that if its descendant was sitting here on this beach in 350 million years' time with a camera around its neck, it would feel that the journey had been worth it. I hoped that it might have a clearer understanding of itself in relation to the world it lived

in. I hoped that it wouldn't be reduced to turning other creatures into horror circus shows in order to try and ensure them their survival. I hoped that if someone tried to feed the remote descendant of a goat to the remote descendant of a dragon for the sake of little more than a shudder of entertainment, that it would feel it was wrong.

I hoped it wouldn't be too chicken to say so.

A mountain gorilla and a twig. This is where all the trouble started.

A ten-foot-long Komodo dragon. The largest currently known to exist is over two feet longer.

Just the saliva of a Komodo dragon can kill a man.

A Komodo dragon sleeping headfirst in a large burrow. It is a very, very, very bad idea to even think of pulling its tail.

A northern white rhino explaining to a hyena that it wishes to retain the rest of its tail.

A silverback mountain gorilla, contemplating.

A silverback mountain gorilla. It is popularly believed that only the leader of a gorilla group develops a silver back due to the burdens of family responsibility, but in fact the backs of most males turn silver after they reach maturity.

Bill Black's helicopter, perched jauntily over a precipice.

Fiordland, New Zealand: The sort of landscape that makes you want to burst into spontaneous applause.

A number of Gothic cathedrals dropped from a considerable height.

LEOPARD-SKIN PILLBOX HAT

E STARTLED OUR-
selves by arriving in Zaïre on a missionary flight, which had
not been our original intention. All regular flights in and out
of Kinshasa had been disrupted by an outbreak of vicious
bickering between Zaïre and its ex-colonial masters, the Belgians, and only a series of nifty moves by Mark, telexing
through the night from Godalming, had secured us this back-
door route into the country via Nairobi.

We had come to find rhinoceroses: northern white rhinoceroses, of which there were about twenty-two left in Zaïre,
and eight in Czechoslovakia. The ones in Czechoslovakia are
not in the wild, of course, and are only there because of the
life's work of a fanatical Czech northern white rhinoceros
collector earlier in this century. There is also a small number
in the San Diego Zoo in California. We had decided to go to

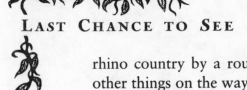

rhino country by a roundabout route in order to see some other things on the way.

The aircraft was a sixteen-seater, filled by the three of us —Mark, Chris Muir (our BBC sound engineer), and myself —and thirteen missionaries. Well, not thirteen actual missionaries, but a mixture of missionaries, mission school teachers, and an elderly American couple who were merely very interested in mission work, and wore straw hats from Miami, cameras, and vacantly benign expressions which they bestowed on everyone indiscriminately, whether they wanted them or not.

We had spent about two hours in the glaring sun creeping sleepily around the dilapidated customs and immigration offices in a remote corner of Nairobi's Wilson airport, trying to spot which was to be our plane and who were to be our traveling companions. It's hard to identify a missionary from first principles, but there was clearly something odd going on because the only place to sit was a small three-seater bench shaded from the sun by the overhanging roof, and everybody was so busy giving up their places on it to everybody else that in the end it simply remained empty and we all stood blinking and wilting in the burgeoning morning heat. After an hour of this, Chris muttered something Scottish under his breath, put down his equipment, lay down on the empty bench, and went to sleep until the flight was ready. I wished I'd thought of it myself.

I knew from many remarks he had made that Mark had a particular dislike of missionaries, whom he has encountered in the field many times in Africa and Asia, and he seemed to be particularly tense and taciturn as we made our way out across the hot tarmac and took our tiny, cramped seats. I then became rather tense myself as the plane started to taxi out to the runway, because the preflight talk from our pilot included a description of our route, an explanation of the safety features of the aircraft, and also a short prayer.

I wasn't disturbed so much by the "O Lord, we thank Thee

for the blessing of this Thy day," but "We commend our lives into Thy hands, O Lord" is frankly not the sort of thing you want to hear from a pilot as his hand is reaching for the throttle. We hurtled down the runway with white knuckles, and as we climbed into the air, we passed a big, old, cigar-fat Dakota finally coming in to land, as if it had been delayed by bad weather over the Great Rift Valley for about thirty years.

In contradiction of everything sensible we know about geography and geometry, the sky over Kenya is simply much bigger than it is anywhere else. As you are lifted up into it, the sense of limitless immensity spreading beneath you to infinitely distant horizons, overwhelms you with excited dread.

The atmosphere on board the plane, on the other hand, was so claustrophobically nice it made you want to spit. Everyone was nice, everyone smiled, everyone laughed that terribly benign fading-away kind of laugh that sets your teeth on edge, and everyone, strangely enough, wore glasses. And not merely glasses. They nearly all had the same sort of glasses, with rims that were black at the top and transparent at the bottom, such as only English vicars, chemistry teachers, and, well, missionaries wear. We sat and behaved ourselves.

I find it very hard not to hum tunelessly when I'm trying to behave myself, and this caused, I think, a certain amount of annoyance in the missionary sitting next to me, which he signaled by doing that terribly benign fading-away kind of laugh at me till I wanted to bite him.

I certainly don't like the idea of missionaries. In fact, the whole business fills me with fear and alarm. I don't believe in God, or at least not in the one we've invented for ourselves in England to fulfill our peculiarly English needs, and certainly not in the ones they've invented in America, who supply their servants with toupees, television stations, and, most important, toll-free telephone numbers. I wish that people

who did believe in such things would keep them to themselves and not export them to the developing world. I sat watching the Miami hats as they gazed out of the window at Africa—between an immensity of land and an immensity of sky they sat there, incomprehensible, smiling at a continent. I think Conrad said something similar about a boat.

They smiled at Mount Kenya, beamed at Mount Kilimanjaro, and were winsomely benign at the whole of the Great Rift Valley as it slid majestically past beneath us. They were even terribly pleased and happy about coming in to land for a brief stop in Mwanza, Tanzania, which is more, as it turned out, than we were.

The aircraft trundled to a halt outside a sort of bus shelter which served Mwanza as an airport, and we were told we had to disembark for half an hour and go and wait in the "international transit lounge."

This consisted of a large concrete shed with two fair-sized rooms in it connected by a corridor. The building had a kind of bombed appearance to it—some of the walls were badly crushed and had tangles of rusty iron spilling from their innards and through the elderly travel posters of Italy pasted over them. We moved in for half an hour, hefted our bags of camera equipment to the floor, and slumped over the battered plastic seats. I dug out a cigarette and Mark dug out his Nikon F3 and MD4 motordrive to photograph me smoking it. There was little else to do.

After a moment or two a man in brown polyester looked in at us, did not at all like the look of us, and asked us if we were transit passengers. We said we were. He shook his head with infinite weariness and told us that if we were transit passengers, then we were supposed to be in the other of the two rooms. We were obviously very crazy and stupid not to have realised this. He stayed there slumped against the doorjamb, raising his eyebrows pointedly at us until we eventually gathered our gear together and dragged it off down the corridor to the other room. He watched us go past him, shaking his head in wonder and sorrow at the stupid futility of the human condition in general and ours in particular, and then closed the door behind us.

The second room was identical to the first. Identical in all respects other than one, which was that it had a hatchway let into one wall. A large vacant-looking girl was leaning through it with her elbows on the counter and her fists jammed up into her cheekbones. She was watching some flies crawling up the wall, not with any great interest because they were not doing anything unexpected, but at least they were doing something. Behind her was a table stacked with biscuits, chocolate bars, cola, and a pot of coffee, and we headed straight toward this like a pack of stoats. Just before we reached it, however, we were suddenly headed off by a man in blue polyester, who asked us what we thought we were doing in there. We explained that we were transit passengers on our way to Zaïre, and he looked at us as if we had completely taken leave of our senses.

"*Transit* passengers?" he said. "It is not allowed for transit passengers to be in here." He waved us magnificently away from the snack counter, made us pick up all our gear again, and herded us back through the door and away into the first room, where a minute later the man in the brown polyester found us again.

He looked at us.

Slow incomprehension engulged him, followed by sadness, anger, deep frustration, and a sense that the world had been created specifically to cause him vexation. He leaned back against the wall, frowned, closed his eyes, and pinched the bridge of his nose.

"You are in the wrong room," he said simply. "You are transit passengers. Please go to the other room."

There is a wonderful calm that comes over you in such situations, particularly when there is a refreshment kiosk involved. We nodded, picked up our gear in a Zen-like manner, and made our way back down the corridor to the second

55
▼▼▼

room. Here the man in blue polyester accosted us once more, but we patiently explained to him that he could fuck off. We needed chocolate, we needed coffee, maybe even a reviving packet of biscuits, and what was more, we intended to have them. We outfaced him, dumped our bags on the ground, walked firmly up to the counter, and hit a major unforeseen snag.

The girl wouldn't sell us anything. She seemed surprised that we even bothered to raise the subject. With her fists still jammed into her cheekbones, she shook her head slowly at us and continued to watch the flies on the wall.

The problem, it gradually transpired after a conversation which flowed like gum from a tree, was this. She would only accept Tanzanian currency. She knew without needing to ask that we didn't have any, for the simple reason that no one ever did. This was an international transit lounge, and the airport had no currency-exchange facilities, therefore no one who came in here could possibly have any Tanzanian currency and therefore she couldn't serve them.

After a few minutes of futile wrangling, we had to accept the flawless simplicity of her argument and just sit out our time there gloomily eyeing the coffee and chocolate bars, while our pockets bulged with useless dollars, sterling, French francs, and Kenyan shillings. The girl stared vacantly at the flies, obviously resigned to the fact that she never did any business at all. After a while we became quite interested in watching the flies as well.

At last we were told that our flight was ready to depart again, and we returned to our planeload of missionaries.

Where, we wondered, had they been while all this had been going on? We didn't ask. After an hour or so we landed at last at Bukavu, and as we taxied up to the terminal shacks of the airport, the plane resounded to happy cries of "Oh, how wonderful, the bishop's come to meet us!" And there he was, big and beaming in his purple tunic, wearing glasses with frames that were black at the top and transparent at the bottom. The missionaries, the mission school teachers, and the American couple who were merely very interested in missionary work climbed smiling out of the plane, and we, pausing to pull our camera bags out from under our seats, followed them.

We were in Zaïre.

I think the best way of explaining what goes so hideously wrong with Zaïre is to reproduce a card we were given by a tourist officer a few days later.

One section of it was written in English, and is for the benefit of the tourist. It goes like this:

Madam, Sir,
On behalf of the President-Founder of the MPR, President of the Republic, of his government and of my fellow citizens, it is agreeable for me to wish you a wonderful sojourn in the Republic of Zaïre.

In this country you will discover majestic sites, a luxuriant flora and an exceptional fauna.

The kindness and hospitality of the Zaïrean people will facilitate your knowledge of the tradition and folklore.

Our young nation expects much from your suggestions and thanks you for your contribution in helping it to welcome the friends you will send us in a much better way.
Minister of E.C.N.T.

That seems fair enough. It's the other section that makes you begin to worry a bit about what you might in fact find. You are meant to show it to any Zaïrois you actually meet, and it goes like this:

Zaïreans, Help Our Visitors

The friend holding this card is visiting our country. He is our guest. If he wants to take photographs, be polite and friendly to him. Do your best to have him enjoy his sojourn, and he will come back, bringing his friends with him.

By helping him, you help your country. Never forget that
tourism provides us with returns which allow us to create
new jobs, to build schools, hospitals, factories, etc.

On the welcome that our guest would have received will
depend our touristic future.

It's alarming enough that an exhortation like this should
be thought to be necessary, but what is even more worrying
is that this section is written only in English.

No "Zaïrean"—or Zaïrois, as they actually call themselves—speaks English, or hardly any do.

The system by which Zaïre works, and which this card
was a wonderfully hopeless attempt to correct, is very simple.
Every official you encounter will make life as unpleasant as
he possibly can until you pay him to stop it. In U.S. dollars.
He then passes you on to the next official, who will be unpleasant to you all over again. By the end of our trip, this
process would assume nightmarish proportions, by comparison with which our entry into Zaïre was a relatively gentle
softening-up process, and only consisted of two hours of rain
and misery in huts.

The first thing we saw in the customs hut was a picture
which gave us a clue about how our expedition to find endangered wildlife in Zaïre was going to go. It was a portrait
of a leopard. That is, it was a portrait of part of a leopard.
The part of the leopard in question had been fashioned into
a rather natty leopard-skin pillbox hat which adorned the
head of Marshall Mobutu Sese Seko Kuku Ngbendu Wa Za
Banga, the President of the Republic of Zaïre, who gazed
down on us with a magisterial calm while his officials got to
work on us.

One was a large and fairly friendly man who occasionally
offered us cigarettes, and the other was a small nasty man
who kept on stealing ours. This is, of course, the classic
interrogation method, designed to bring the victim to the
brink of pathetic emotional breakdown. It's obviously a tech-

nique they learned somewhere and have just found the habit hard to break, even though all they actually wanted to know from us was our names, passport numbers, and the serial numbers of every single piece of equipment we had with us.

The big man in particular seemed to wish us no personal ill as he guided us gently through the insanity to which it was his duty to subject us, and I came to recognise a feeling I've heard described, when oddly close and touching relationships develop between torturers and their victims or kidnappers and their hostages. There is a feeling of all being in this together. The forms we had to fill in were headed "Belgian Congo," crossed out, with "Zaïre" written in in pencil, which meant that they had to be at least eighteen years old. The only form they didn't seem to have was the only one we actually wanted. We had been warned by friends that we had to get ourselves a currency-declaration form when we entered Zaïre or we would hit trouble later on. We repeatedly asked for one, but they said they had run out. They said we could get one in Goma and that would be all right.

They toyed with the idea of confiscating my Cambridge Z88 laptop computer just in case we were planning to overthrow the government with it, but in the end the small nasty man merely confiscated Chris's car magazine on the grounds that he liked cars and then, for now, we were free.

We went into the town of Bukavu in a sort of taxi-like thing. The town turned out to be an enormous distance from the airport, probably at the insistence of the taxi drivers. As we bounded along the appallingly rutted road that followed the margin of the lake and along which a significant proportion of the population of Zaïre seemed to be walking, our driver kept on diving beneath the dashboard of the car for long periods at a time. I watched this with some alarm, which was severely increased when I eventually worked out what he was doing. He was operating the clutch by hand. I won-

59
▼▼▼

dered whether to mention this to the others but decided that, no, it would only worry them. Mark later mentioned that we had not passed any other motor vehicles at all on the drive, except for a couple of trucks which had been parked for so long that they no longer had any rear axles. I didn't notice this myself, because once I had identified what the driver was doing with the clutch, I simply kept my eyes closed for the remainder of the journey.

When at last we arrived at the hotel, which was surprisingly airy and spacious for such a dilapidated town as Bukavu, we were rattled and exhausted and we started to yawn at one another a lot. This was a kind of unspoken code for being fed up with the sight of one another despite the fact that it was only six in the evening. We each went off to our respective rooms and sat in our separate heaps.

I sat by the window and watched as the sun began to go down over the lake, the name of which I couldn't remember because all the maps were in Mark's room. From this vantage point, Bukavu looked quite idyllic, situated on a peninsula which jutted into the lake. Lake Kivu. I remembered the name now. I was still feeling very jangled and jittery and decided that staring at the lake a bit might help.

It was placid and silvery, shading to grey in the distance where it met the fading shapes of the hills that surrounded it. That helped.

The early-evening light cast long shadows over the old Belgian colonial houses that were stepped down the hill from the hotel, huddled about with bright blossoms and palm trees. That was good too. Even the green corrugated roofs of the cruder new buildings were soothed by the light. I watched the black kites wheeling out over the water and found that I was calming down. I got up and started to unpack the things I needed for the night, and at last a wonderful sense of peace and well-being settled on me, disturbed only by the sudden realisation that I had once again left my toothpaste in last night's hotel. And my writing paper. And my cigarette lighter. I decided it was time to explore the town.

The main street was a grim hill, wide, disheveled, and strewn with rubbish. The shops were for the most part concrete and dingy, and because Zaïre is an ex-Belgian colony, every other shop is a *pharmacie,* just like in Belgium and France, except that none of them, as it happened, sold toothpaste, which bewildered me.

Most of the other shops were in fact impossible to identify. When a shop appeared to sell a mixture of ghetto blasters, socks, soap, and chickens, it didn't seem unreasonable to go in and ask if they had any toothpaste or paper stuck away on one of their shelves as well, but they looked at me as if I was completely mad. Couldn't I see that this was a ghetto blaster, socks, soap, and chicken shop? Eventually, after trailing up and down the street for half a mile in either direction, I found both of them at a tiny street stall which also turned out to sell ballpoint pens, airmail envelopes, and cigarette lighters, and in fact seemed to be so peculiarly attuned to my needs that I was tempted to ask if they had a copy of *New Scientist* as well.

I then realised that most of the essentials of life were available out on the street. Photocopying, for example. Here and there along the street were rickety trestle tables with big old photocopiers on them, and once or twice I was hailed by a street hustler and asked if I wanted to have something photocopied or sleep with his sister. I returned to the hotel, wrote some notes on the writing paper, which for some reason was pink, and slept as if I were dead.

The following morning we flew to the town of Goma. Here we discovered that even when making internal flights in Zaïre you still had to go through the full rigmarole of immigration and customs controls all over again. We were held under armed guard while a large and thuggish airport official

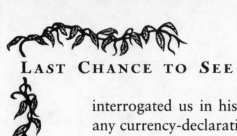

interrogated us in his office as to why we hadn't acquired any currency-declaration forms at Bukavu.

The fact that they hadn't had any currency-declaration forms to give us at Bukavu cut no ice with him.

"Fifty dollars," he said.

His office was large and bare and contained just one small desk with two sheets of paper in a drawer. He leaned back and stared at the ceiling, which had obviously seen a lot of this sort of thing going on. Then he leaned forward again and pulled the palms of his hands slowly down over his face as if he were trying to peel it off. He said again, "Fifty dollars. Each," and then stared idly at the corner of his desk and rolled a pencil slowly in his fingers. We were subjected to an hour of this before he finally tired of our appalling French and let us go. We hadn't paid.

We emerged blinking from the airport and, miraculously, met up with the driver whom some friends of Mark's had arranged to take us up into the Virunga volcanoes, where the mountain gorillas lived.

The gorillas were not the animals we had come to Zaïre to look for. It is very hard, however, to come all the way to Zaïre and not go and see them. I was going to say that this is because they are our closest living relatives, but I'm not sure that that's an appropriate reason. Generally, in my experience, when you visit a country in which you have any relatives living, there's a tendency to want to lie low and hope they don't find out you're in town. At least with the gorillas, you know that there's no danger of having to go out to dinner with them and catch up on several million years of family history, so you can visit them with impunity. They are, of course, only collateral relatives—nth cousins, n times removed. We are both descended from a common ancestor, who is, sadly, no longer with us, and who has, since Darwin's day, been the subject of endless speculation as to what manner of creature he/she was.

The section of the primate family of which we are members (rich, successful members of the family, the ones who made good and who should, by any standards, be looking after the other, less well-off members of the family) are the great apes—we are great apes.

The other great apes are the gorillas (of which there are three subspecies: mountain, eastern lowland, and western lowland), two species of chimpanzee, and the orangutans of Borneo and Sumatra. Of these, the most closely related are the gorillas, the chimps, and us. We and the gorillas separated on the evolutionary tree more recently than we did from the other great apes, so the gorillas are more closely related to us than they are to the orangutans. We are very, very close relatives indeed—as close to each other as the Indian elephant and the African elephant, which also share a common, extinct ancestor.

The Virunga volcanoes, where the mountain gorillas live, straddle the border of Zaïre, Rwanda, and Uganda. There are about 280 gorillas there, roughly two-thirds of which live in Zaïre, and the other third in Rwanda. I say roughly, because the gorillas are not yet sufficiently advanced in evolutionary terms to have discovered the benefits of passports, currency-declaration forms, and official bribery, and therefore tend to wander backward and forward across the border as and when their beastly, primitive whim takes them. A few stragglers even pop over into Uganda from time to time, but there are no gorillas actually living there as permanent residents because the Ugandan part of the Virungas only covers about twenty-five square kilometres, and is unprotected and full of people whom the gorillas, given the choice, would rather steer clear of.

The drive from Goma takes about five hours, and we made the hastiest departure we could manage after two and a half hours of serious madness with a ticket agent, a hotel manager, a lunch break, and one of the larger national banks, which it would be tedious to relate, but not half as tedious as it was to undergo.

Things hit a limit, though, when I was set upon by a pick-pocket in a baker's shop.

I didn't notice that I was being set upon by a pickpocket, which I am glad of, because I like to work only with professionals. Everybody else in the shop did notice, however, and the man was hurriedly manhandled away and ejected into the street while I was still busy choosing buns. The baker tried to tell me what had happened, but my Zaïrois French wasn't up to it and I thought he was merely recommending the curranty ones, of which I therefore bought six.

Mark arrived at that moment with some tinned pears, our gorilla permits, and our driver, who quickly understood what was going on and explained to me what had happened. He also explained that the currant buns were no good, but said we might as well keep them because none of the others were any good either and we had to have something. He was a tall, rangy Muslim with an engaging smile, and he responded very positively to the suggestion that we should now get the hell out of here.

When people talk of "darkest Africa," it's usually Zaïre they have in mind. This is the land of jungles, mountains, enormous rivers, volcanoes, more exotic wildlife than you'd be wise to shake a stick at, hunter-gatherer pygmies who are still largely untouched by Western civilisation and one of the worst transport systems anywhere in the world. This is the Africa in which Stanley presumed to meet Dr. Livingstone.

Until the nineteenth century this enormous tract of Africa was simply a large black hole in the centre of any European map of the dark continent, and it was only after Livingstone's penetration of the interior that the black hole began to exercise any gravitational effect on the outside world.

The first people to pour in were the missionaries: Catholics who arrived to teach the native populace that the Protestants were wrong and Protestants who came to teach that the Catholics were wrong. The only thing the Protestants and

Catholics agreed on was that the natives had been wrong for two thousand years.

The missionaries were closely followed by traders in search of slaves, ivory, copper, and suitable land on which plantations could be established. With the help of Stanley, who was on a five-year contract to open up the interior of Africa, King Leopold of the Belgians successfully laid claim to this vast region in 1885 and promptly subjected its inhabitants to an exceptionally brutal and ruthless form of colonisation, thus giving them a practical and convincing demonstration of what "wrong" actually meant.

When news of the worst atrocities leaked to the outside world, Leopold was forced to hand over "his" land to the Belgian government, who took it upon themselves to do virtually nothing about it. But by the 1950s independence movements were sweeping across Africa and, after riots and appalling massacres in the capital of Kinshasa in 1959, the colonial authorities were shaken so badly that they granted independence the following year. The country eventually changed its name from the Belgian Congo to Zaïre in 1971.

Zaïre, incidentally, is about eighty times the size of Belgium.

Like most colonies, Zaïre had imposed on it a stifling bureaucracy, the sole function of which was to refer decisions upward to its colonial masters. Local officials rarely had the power to do things, only to prevent them from being done until bribed. So once the colonial masters are removed, the bureaucracy continues to thrash around like a headless chicken with nothing to do but trip itself up, bump into things, and, when it can get the firepower, shoot itself in the foot. You can always tell an ex-colony from the inordinate numbers of people who are able to find employment stopping anybody who has anything to do from doing it.

Five hours of sleepy bumping in the van brought us to Bukima, a village in the foothills of the Virungas which

marks the point where the road finally gives up, and from which we had to travel on by foot.

Set a little way above the village, in front of a large square, was an absurdly grand ex-colonial building, empty except for an absurdly small office tucked into the back where a small man in an Army uniform pored over our gorilla permits with a grim air of bemusement, as if he'd never seen one before, or at least not for well over an hour. He then occupied himself with a shortwave radio for a few minutes before turning to us and saying that he knew exactly who we were, had been expecting us, and that because of our contacts with the World Wildlife Fund in Nairobi, he was going to allow us an extra day with the gorillas, and who the hell were we anyway, and why had no one told him we were coming?

This seemed, on the face of it, to be unanswerable, so we left him to try and figure it out for himself while we went to look for some porters to help us with our baggage for the three-hour walk up to the warden's hut, where we were to spend the night. They weren't hard to find. There was a large band of them gathered hopefully around our van and our driver was eager to know how many we needed to carry all our bags. He seemed to emphasise the word *all* rather strongly.

There was a sudden moment of horrible realisation. We had been so keen to clear out of Goma as fast as possible that we had forgotten a major part of our plan, which was to leave the bulk of our gear at a hotel in town. As a result of this oversight, we had more baggage with us than we actually needed to carry up to the gorillas.

A lot more.

As well as basic gorilla-watching kit—jeans, T-shirt, a sort of waterproof thing, a ton of cameras, and tins of pears— there was also an immense store of dirty laundry, a suit and shoes for meeting my French publisher in Paris, aftershave, a dozen computer magazines, a thesaurus, half the collected works of Dickens, and a large wooden model of a Komodo dragon. I believe in traveling light, but then I also believe I should give up smoking and shop early for Christmas.

Hiding our considerable embarrassment, we chose a team of porters to carry this little lot up into the Virunga volcanoes for us. They didn't mind. If we were prepared to pay them to carry Dickens and aftershave up to the gorillas and back down again, then they were perfectly happy to do it. White men have done much worse things in Zaïre than that, but maybe not much sillier.

The trek up to the visitors' hut was strenuous, and involved plenty of stops for sharing our cigarettes and Coca-Cola with the bearers, while they frequently redistributed the bags of Dickens and computer magazines among themselves and experimented with different and novel methods of keeping them on their heads.

For much of the time we were tramping through wet fields of sago, and a foolish but happy thought suddenly occurred to me. We were walking through the only known anagram of my name—which is Sago Mud Salad. I speculated footlingly as to what possible cosmic significance there could be to this, and by the time I had finally dismissed the thought, the light was fading and we had arrived at the hut, which was a fairly spartan wooden building, but new and quite well built.

A damp and heavy mist hung over the land, almost obscuring the distant volcano peaks. The evening was unexpectedly cold, and we spent it by the light of hissing Tilley lamps, eating our tinned pears and our single remaining bun, and talking in broken French to our two guides, whose names were Murara and Serundori.

These were magnificently smooth characters dressed in military camouflage and black berets who slouched across the table languidly caressing their rifles. They explained that the reason for the getup was that they were ex-commandos. All guides had to carry rifles, they told us, partly as protection against the wildlife, but more importantly in case they

encountered poachers. Murara told us that he had personally shot dead five poachers. He explained with a shrug that there was *pas de problème* about it. No bother with inquests or anything like that, he just shot them and went home.

He sat back in his chair and idly fingered the rifle sight while we toyed nervously with our pear halves.

Poaching of one kind or another is, of course, the single most serious threat to the survival of the mountain gorillas, but it's hard not to wonder whether declaring open season on human beings is the best plan for solving the problem. We are not an endangered species ourselves yet, but this is not for lack of trying.

In fact, the poaching problem itself is declining—or at least parts of it are. Four in every five of the gorillas alive in the world's zoos today were originally taken from the wild, but no public zoo would accept a gorilla now, except from another zoo, since it would be a bit difficult to explain where it came from. There is still a demand for them from private collectors, however, and the unprotected Ugandan part of the Virungas is still a weak link. In September 1988 an infant was captured on the Ugandan side: two adult members of its family were shot dead and the young animal was later sold to Rwandan smugglers by a game warden (now in prison) for about twenty-five thousand dollars. This is the most destructive aspect of this sort of poaching: for every young gorilla captured, several other members of its family will probably die trying to protect it.

Worse than those who want to collect gorillas for their private zoos are those who just want to collect bits of gorillas. For many years there was a brisk trade in skulls and hands that were sold to tourists and expatriates who mistakenly thought they would look finer on their mantelpieces than they did on the original gorilla. This, thank goodness, is also now declining, since a taste for bone-headed brutality is now held to be less of a social grace than formerly.

In some parts of Africa gorillas are still killed for food,

though not in the Virunga volcanoes—at least, not deliberately. The problem is that many other animals are, and gorillas very frequently get caught in traps set for bushbuck or duiker. A young female gorilla called Jozi, for example, caught her hand in a wire antelope snare and eventually died of septicemia in August 1988. So to protect the gorillas, antipoaching patrols are still necessary.

There were two other people sharing our hut that evening. They were a couple of German students whose names I appear now to have forgotten, but since they were indistinguishable from all the other German students we encountered from time to time on our trips, I will simply call them Helmut and Kurt.

Helmut and Kurt were young, fair-haired, vigorous, incredibly well-equipped, and much better than us at virtually everything. We saw very little of them during the early part of the evening because they were very busy preparing their meal. This involved constructing some kind of brick oven outside, and then doing a lot of coming and going with bowls of boiling water, stopwatches, penknives, and dismembered bits of the local wildlife. Eventually they sat and ate their feast in front of us with grim efficiency and an insulting refusal to make any disparaging glances at all in the direction of our tinned pear halves.

Then they said they were going to bed for the night, only they weren't going to sleep in the hut because they had a tent with them, which was much better. It was a German tent. They nodded us a curt good night and left.

In bed that night, after I had lain awake for a while worrying about Murara and Serundori's casual propensity for shooting people, I turned to worrying instead about Helmut and Kurt. If they were going to be like that, then I just wished they hadn't been German. It was too easy. Too obvious. It was like coming across an Irishman who actually was stupid, a mother-in-law who actually was fat, or an American businessman who actually did have a middle initial and smoke a

69
▼▼▼

cigar. You feel as if you are unwillingly performing in a music-hall sketch and wishing you could rewrite the script. If Helmut and Kurt had been Brazilian or Chinese or Latvian or anything else at all, they could then have behaved in exactly the same way and it would have been surprising and intriguing and, more to the point from my perspective, much easier to write about. Writers should not be in the business of propping up stereotypes. I wondered what to do about it, decided that they could simply *be* Latvians if I wanted, and then at last drifted off peacefully to worrying about my boots.

Mark had told me before we went to bed that when I woke up the first thing I had to remember was to turn my boots upside-down and shake them.

I asked him why.

"Scorpions," he replied. "Good night."

Early in the morning Murara and Serundori were waiting at the hut door fondling their rifles and machetes, and wearing meaningful glints in their eyes that we weren't at all certain we liked. However, they had good news for us. Since gorillas tend not to make their personal arrangements to suit the convenience of visiting collateral relatives, they were sometimes to be found up to eight hours' trek away from the visitors' hut. Today, however, the news was that they were only about an hour's distance from us, so we would have an easy day of it. We gathered together our gorilla-watching gear, carefully leaving behind the aftershave, the Dickens, and also our flash guns, on the assumption that these were all things that would, to differing degrees, upset the gorillas, said good morning to Helmut and Kurt, who were joining us for the expedition, and set off together in search of the gorillas. Ahead of us through the misty morning light reared the hump of Mikeno volcano.

The forest we plunged into was thick and wet and I complained about this to Mark.

He explained that gorillas like to live in montane rain forest, or cloud forest. It was over ten thousand feet above sea level, above the cloud level, and always damp. Water drips off the trees the whole time.

"It's not at all like lowland primary rain forest," said Mark, "more like secondary rain forest, which is what you get when primary forest is burned or cut down."

"I thought that the whole problem with rain forest was that it wouldn't grow again when you cut it down," I said.

"You won't get primary rain forest again. Well, you might, we don't know. You might get it over hundreds or thousands of years. It certainly takes a hell of a lot longer than we've been keeping records for. And all of the original wildlife will have disappeared for good, of course.

"Primary rain forest is an incredibly complex system, but when you're actually standing in it, it looks half-empty. In its mature state you get a very high, thick canopy of leaves, because of all the trees competing with each other to get at the sunlight. But since little light penetrates this canopy, there will tend to be very little vegetation at ground level. Instead you get an ecological system which is the most complex of any on earth, and it's all designed to disseminate energy the trees have absorbed from the sun throughout the whole forest.

"Cloud forest, like this, is much simpler. The trees are much lower and more spaced out, so there is plenty of ground-cover vegetation as well, all of which the gorillas like very much because it means they can hide. And there's plenty of food within arm's reach."

For us, however, all the thick, wet vegetation made the forest hard work to fight through. Murara and Serundori swung their machetes so casually through the almost impenetrable undergrowth that it took me a while to begin to see that there was more to it than just vague hacking.

Machetes are a very specific shape, a little like the silhouette of a banana with a fattened end. Every part of the blade

71
▼▼▼

has a slightly different curve or angle of cut to the line of movement, and a different weight behind it as well. It was fascinating to watch the instinctive ways in which, from one slash to another, the guides would adapt their stroke to the exact type of vegetation they were trying to cut through—one moment it would be a thick branch, another moment it would be banks of nettles, and another moment tangled hanging vines. It was like a very casual game of tennis played by highly skilled players.

Not only was the forest thick, it was also cold, wet, and full of large black ants that bit all of us except for Helmut and Kurt, who were wearing special antproof socks which they had brought with them from Latvia.

We complimented them on their foresight and they shrugged and said it was nothing. Latvians were always well prepared. They looked at our recording equipment and said that they were surprised that we thought it was adequate. They had much better tape recorders than that in Latvia. We said that that might very well be so, but that we were very happy with it and the BBC seemed to think it was fine for the job. Helmut (or was it Kurt?) explained that they had much better broadcasting corporations in Latvia.

The outbreak of outright hostilities was happily averted at this moment by a signal from our guides to keep quiet. We were near the gorillas.

"But of course," said Kurt, with a slight smile playing along his thin Latvian lips, as if he'd known all the while that this was exactly where the gorillas would be.

But it wasn't a gorilla itself that had attracted our guides' attention, it was a gorilla's bed. By the side of the track along which we were walking there was a large depression in the undergrowth where a gorilla had been sleeping for the night. Plant stems had been pulled down and folded under to keep the gorilla off the ground, which was cold and damp at night.

One of the characteristics that laymen find most odd about zoologists is their insatiable enthusiasm for animal droppings. I can understand, of course, that the droppings yield a great deal of information about the habits and diets of the animals concerned, but nothing quite explains the sheer glee that the actual objects seem to inspire.

A sharp yelp of joy told me that Mark had found some. He dropped to his knees and started to fire off his Nikon at a small pile of gorilla dung.

"It's in the nest," he explained once he had finished, "which is very interesting, you see. The mountain gorillas, the ones that live here, actually defecate in their nests because it's too cold to get up at night. The western lowland gorillas, on the other hand, don't. They live in a warmer climate, so getting up in the middle of the night is less of a problem. Also, the western lowland gorillas live on a diet of fruit, which is another incentive for not shitting in their nests."

"I see," I said.

Helmut started to say something, which I like to think was probably something about having far superior types of gorilla dung in Latvia, but I interrupted him because I suddenly had one of those strange, uncanny feelings that I was being watched by a truck.

We kept very quiet and looked very carefully around us. There was nothing we could see near us, nothing in the trees above us, nothing peering furtively from the bushes. It was a moment or two before we saw anything at all, but then at last a slight movement caught our eyes. About thirty yards away down the track we were following, standing in plain view, was something so big that we hadn't even noticed it. It was a mountain gorilla, or perhaps I should say a gorilla mountain, standing propped up on its front knuckles so that it assumed the shape of a large and muscular sloping-ridge tent.

You will have heard it said before that these creatures are awesome beasts, and I would like to add my own particular perception to this: these creatures are awesome beasts. It is hard to know how better to put it. A kind of humming

73
▼▼▼

mental paralysis grips you when you first encounter a creature such as this in the wild, and indeed there is no creature such as this. All sorts of wild and vertiginous feelings well up into your brain that you seem to have no connection with and no name for, perhaps because it is thousands or millions of years since such feelings were last aroused.

I'm going to be a bit fanciful for a moment, because it is very hard not to be when your rational, civilised brain (I use the words in the loosest possible sense) experiences things it has no way of recognising or accounting for but which are nevertheless very powerful.

I've heard an idea proposed, I've no idea how seriously, to account for the sensation of vertigo. It's an idea that I instinctively like and it goes like this.

The dizzy sensation we experience when standing in high places is not simply a fear of falling. It's often the case that the only thing likely to make us fall is the actual dizziness itself, so it is, at best, an extremely irrational, even self-fulfilling fear. However, in the distant past of our evolutionary journey toward our current state, we lived in trees. We leapt from tree to tree. There are even those who speculate that we may have something birdlike in our ancestral line. In which case, there may be some part of our mind that, when confronted with a void, expects to be able to leap out into it and even urges us to do so. So what you end up with is a conflict between a primitive, atavistic part of your mind which is saying, "Jump!" and the more modern, rational part of your mind which is saying, *"For Christ's sake, don't!"*

Certainly the dizzy experience of vertigo seems to have far more in common with feelings of oscillating mental conflict and confusion than it does with simple fear. If it is a fear, it's one we love to play with and tease ourselves with, which is how designers of big dippers and Ferris wheels make a living.

The feeling I had looking at my first silverback gorilla in the wild was vertiginous. It was as if there was something I was meant to do, some reaction that was expected of me, and I didn't know what it was or how to do it. My modern mind was simply saying, "Run away!" but all I could do was stand, trembling, and stare. The right moment seemed to slip away and fall into an unbridgeable gulf between us, and left me simply gawping helplessly on my side. The gorilla, meanwhile, seemed to notice that we had been busy photographing its dung and merely stalked off into the undergrowth.

We set off to follow it, but it was in its own element and we were not. We were not even able to tell whereabouts in its own element it was, and after a while we gave up and started to explore the area more generally again.

The gorilla we had seen was a large male silverback. "Silverback" simply means that its back was silver, or grey-haired. Only the backs of males turn silver, and it happens after the male has reached maturity. Tradition has it that only the chief male of a group will develop a silver back, and that it will happen within days, or even hours, of it taking over as leader, but this apparently is nonsense. Popular and beguiling nonsense, but nonsense. And while we are on the subject of nonsense, I should mention something that we discovered a few days later when talking to Conrad Aveling, a field researcher in Goma who has for years been responsible for gorilla conservation work in the area.

We told Conrad how alarmed we had been by Murara and Serundori's accounts of simply going out and mowing down the local poachers, and he sat back in his chair, kicked up his heels, and roared with laughter.

"It's incredible what these guys will tell the tourists! I bet they told you they were ex-commandos as well, did they?"

We admitted, rather sheepishly, that they had. Conrad clasped his hand to his brow and shook his head.

"The only thing about them that's ex-commando," he said, "is their uniforms. They buy them off the commandos. The commandos sell them to buy food because they hardly ever get paid. It's all complete nonsense. I heard another great story the other day. A tourist had asked a guide—and

75
▼▼▼

this was at Rawindi, where there are no gorillas—the tourist asked, 'What happens when a gorilla meets a lion?' and instead of answering, 'Well, that's a silly question, because lions and gorillas live in completely different areas and would never ever meet,' the guide obviously feels obliged to think of some sort of colourful answer. So he says, 'What happens is that the gorilla beats the hell out of the lion, then wraps his body in leaves and twigs and then stamps on him.' I only heard about it myself because the tourist came to me afterward and said how fascinated he had been to hear about it. It bothers me when they make up these colourful answers. I wish I could make them understand that if they don't know the answer, or they think the right answer isn't very interesting, it's better to say so rather than just invent absolute nonsense."

One thing that was beyond dispute, however, was that when our guides were not inventing stuff or acting out Rambo fantasies, they really knew the forest, and they really knew the gorillas. They had (and Conrad Aveling confirmed all this enthusiastically) themselves "habituated" two of the gorilla groups for human contact. "Habituating" is a very long, complicated, and delicate business, but, briefly, it is the process of contacting a group in the wild and visiting them every day, if you can find them, over a period of months or even years and training them to accept the presence of human beings, so that they can then be studied and also visited by tourists.

The length of time it takes to habituate gorillas depends on the dominant silverback. He's the one whose confidence you have to win. In the case of the family group we were visiting, it took fully three years. Conrad Aveling spent the first eight months of his time on the project crawling around in the undergrowth with them but never actually saw them once, though he was often no more than twenty or thirty feet away.

"One of the problems of habituating in this sort of habitat," he explained, "is that it's so thick you can't see each other, and what happens is you end up having these sudden confrontations at about three or four metres or less, and you *still* can't see each other. Everybody's jumping out of their skin. The gorilla's jumping out of his skin, I'm jumping out of mine. It's extremely exciting. You get a real adrenaline rush. A problem with the Bukavu group was that the silverback wouldn't charge. I actually *wanted* him to, because then, having charged, he would expose himself and then realise that I didn't mean him any harm. But he wouldn't do that, he just kept circling. Usually they do charge, and if they do, you have this face-to-face, and you have a moment to understand that neither of you means the other any harm and the gorilla backs off."

"But you go into a submissive posture, do you?" asked Mark. "You don't confront him?"

"No, I usually don't go into a submissive posture. I'm usually too frightened to move."

Once a silverback accepts humans, the rest of the group will quickly fall into line, and, interestingly enough, any other groups in the area will usually become habituated much more quickly. There is hardly ever any trouble provided everybody treats everybody else with respect. The gorillas are perfectly capable of making it clear when they don't wish to be disturbed. There was one occasion on which a gorilla group had had a particularly stressful morning as a result of an encounter with another gorilla group, and the last thing they wanted was to be bothered with humans in the afternoon, so when a tracker brought some tourists and overstayed his welcome, the silverback took hold of the tracker's hand and gently bit his watch off.

Now, the business of tourism is obviously a vexed one. I had myself wanted to visit the gorillas for years, but had been deterred by the worry that tourism must be disturbing to the gorillas' habitat and way of life. There is also the risk of exposing the gorillas to diseases to which they have no

immunity. It is well known that the famous and extraordinary pioneer of gorilla conservation, Dian Fossey, was for most of her life passionately opposed to tourism and wished to keep the world away from the gorillas. However, she did, reluctantly, change her mind toward the end of her life, and the prevalent view now is that tourism, if it's carefully controlled and monitored, is the one thing that can guarantee the gorillas' survival. The sad but unavoidable fact is that it comes down to simple economics. Without tourists it's only a question of which will happen first—either the gorillas' forest habitat will be entirely destroyed for crop farming and firewood, or the gorillas will be hunted to extinction by poachers. Put at its crudest, the gorillas are now worth more to the locals (and the government) alive than dead.

The restrictions, which are tightly enforced, are these. Each gorilla family can only be visited once a day, usually for about an hour, by a party of a maximum of six people, each of whom are paying a hundred dollars for the privilege. And maybe they won't even get to see the gorillas.

We were lucky; we did. After our first brief encounter with the silverback, it had looked, for a while, as if we would not find any more. We moved slowly and carefully through the undergrowth while Murara and Serundori made regular coughing and grunting noises. The purpose of these was to let the gorillas know we were coming and reassure them that we meant no harm. The noises are imitations of a noise that gorillas themselves make. Apparently it doesn't actually matter much about trying to imitate them, though. It's hardly going to fool anyone. It just reassures the gorillas that you always make the same noise. You could sing the national anthem as far as they are concerned.

Just as we were about to give up and go back, we tried one more turning, and suddenly the forest seemed to be thick with gorillas. A few feet above us a female was lounging in a tree idly stripping the bark off a twig with her teeth. She noticed us but was not interested. Two babies were cavorting recklessly ten feet from the ground in a very slender tree, and a young male was chugging through the undergrowth nearby on the lookout for food. We stared at the two babies in astounded fascination at the wonderful wild abandon with which they were hurling themselves around each other and the terrible meagreness of the tree in which they had elected to do it. It was hard to believe the tree could support them, and indeed it couldn't. They suddenly came crashing down through it, having completely misunderstood the law of gravity, and slunk off sheepishly into the undergrowth.

We followed, encountering one gorilla after another until at last we came across another silverback lying on his side beneath a bush, with his long arm folded up over his head scratching his opposite ear while he watched a couple of leaves doing not very much. It was instantly clear what he was doing. He was contemplating life. He was hanging out. It was quite obvious. Or rather, the temptation to find it quite obvious was absolutely overwhelming.

They look like humans, they move like humans, they hold things in their fingers like humans, the expressions which play across their faces and in their intensely human-looking eyes are expressions that we instinctively feel we recognise as human expressions. We look them in the face and we think, "We know what they're like," but we don't. Or rather, we actually block off any possible glimmering of understanding of what they may be like by making easy and tempting assumptions.

I crept closer to the silverback, slowly and quietly on my hands and knees, till I was about eighteen inches away from him. He glanced around at me unconcernedly, as if I was just someone who had walked into the room, and continued his contemplations. I guessed that the animal was probably about the same height as me—over six feet tall—but I would think about twice as heavy. Mostly muscle, with soft grey-black skin hanging quite loosely on his front, covered in coarse black hair.

As I moved again, he shifted himself away from me, just about six inches, as if I had sat slightly too close to him on a sofa and he was grumpily making a bit more room. Then he lay on his front with his chin on his fist, idly scratching his cheek with his other hand. I sat as quiet and still as I could, despite discovering that I was being bitten to death by ants. The silverback looked from one to another of us without any great concern, and then his attention dropped to his own hands as he idly scratched some flecks of dirt off one of his fingers with his thumb. I had the impression that we were of as much interest to him as a boring Sunday afternoon in front of the television. He yawned.

It's so bloody hard not to anthropomorphise. But these impressions keep on crowding in on you because they spark so much instant recognition, however illusory that recognition may be. It's the only way of conveying what it was *like*.

After a quiet interval had passed, I carefully pulled the pink writing paper out of my bag and started to make the notes that I'm writing from at the moment. This seemed to interest him a little more. I suppose he had simply never seen pink writing paper before. His eyes followed as my hand squiggled across the paper, and after a while he reached out and touched first the paper and then the top of my ballpoint pen—not to take it away from me, or even to interrupt me, just to see what it was and what it felt like. I felt very moved by this, and had a foolish impulse to want to show him my camera as well.

He retreated a little and lay down again about four feet from me, with his fist once more propped under his chin. I loved the extraordinary thoughtfulness of his expression, and the way his lips were bunched together by the upward pressure of his fist. The most disconcerting intelligence seemed to be apparent from the sudden sidelong glances he would give me, prompted not by any particular move I had made but apparently by a thought that had struck him.

I began to feel how patronising it was of us to presume to

80
▼▼▼

judge their intelligence, as if ours was any kind of standard by which to measure. I tried to imagine instead how he saw us, but of course that's almost impossible to do, because the assumptions you end up making as you try to bridge the imaginative gap are, of course, your own, and the most misleading assumptions are the ones you don't even know you're making. I pictured him lying there easily in his own world, tolerating my presence in it, but, I think, possibly sending me signals to which I did not know how to respond. And then I pictured myself beside him, festooned with the apparatus of my intelligence—my Goretex windbreaker, my pen and paper, my autofocus matrix-metering Nikon F4, and my inability to comprehend any of the life we had left behind us in the forest. But somewhere in the genetic history that we each carry with us in every cell of our body was a deep connection with this creature, as inaccessible to us now as last year's dreams, but, like last year's dreams, always invisibly and unfathomably present.

It put me in mind of what I think must be a vague memory of a movie, in which a New Yorker, the son of East European immigrants, goes to find the village that his family originally came from. He is rich and successful and expects to be greeted with excitement, admiration, and wonder.

Instead, he is not exactly rejected, not exactly dismissed, but is welcomed in ways that he is unable to understand. He is disturbed by their lack of reaction to his presence until he realises that their stillness in the face of him is not rejection, but merely a peace that he is welcome to join but not to disturb. The gifts he has brought with him from civilisation turn to dust in his hands as he realises that everything he has is merely the shadow cast by what he has lost.

I watched the gorilla's eyes again, wise and knowing eyes, and wondered about this business of trying to teach apes language. Our language. Why? There are many members of our own species who live in and with the forest and know it and understand it. We don't listen to them. What is there to

suggest we would listen to anything an ape could tell us? Or that it would be able to tell us of its life in a language that hasn't been born of that life? I thought, maybe it is not that they have yet to gain a language, it is that we have lost one.

The silverback seemed at last to tire of our presence. He hauled himself to his feet and lumbered easily off into another part of his home.

On the way back to the hut I discovered that I had a small tin of tuna in my camera bag, so we greedily devoured this on our return, along with a bottle of beer, and that, at two o'clock in the afternoon, marked the end of fun for the day, unless you count listening to a couple of German—sorry, Latvian—students explaining how good their penknives are as fun.

At this, Mark started to get quietly ratty, which meant that he grasped the beer bottle very tightly between his hands and stared at it a lot. Kurt asked us what we were planning to do next and we said we were flying up to Garamba National Park to see if we could find any northern white rhinos. Kurt nodded and said that himself he thought he would probably walk to Uganda tonight.

Mark's knuckles grew white around his beer bottle. Mark, like most zoologists, tends to prefer animals to people anyway, but in this case I was with him all the way. It occurred to me that we had spent a day rapt with wonder watching the mountain gorillas, and being particularly moved at how human they seemed, and finding this to be one of their most engaging and fascinating features. To find afterward that a couple of hours spent with actual humans was merely irritating was a bit confusing.

Three days later I found myself standing on top of a termite hill staring at another termite hill through binoculars.

I knew that what I was standing on was a termite hill, but was disappointed that the thing I was staring at was not a northern white rhinoceros, since we had been walking determinedly toward it for upwards of an hour in the blazing midday sun in the middle of what can only be described as Africa.

Also we had run out of water. I could scarcely believe, having been brought up on a rich diet of H. Rider Haggard, Noël Coward, and *The Eagle,* that the first thing I would do on encountering the actual real savannah plains of Africa was to march straight out into them in the midday sun and run out of water.

Though I wouldn't admit it, of course, having been brought up on a rich diet of H. Rider Haggard, etc., I was actually a bit frightened. The point about not running out of water in the middle of the savannah is that you do actually need the stuff. Your body regularly mentions to you that you need it, and after a while becomes quite strident on the subject. Furthermore, we were miles from anywhere, and though there were a number of theories flying around about where we'd left the Landrover, none of them so far had stood up to rigorous testing.

I don't know how worried Mark or Chris were at this point, because it was difficult to get them—particularly Chris—to say anything coherent. Chris is from Edinburgh, and is an excellent specimen of one of the northern races: red-haired and fair-skinned, never happier than when carrying a DAT recorder and a microphone wrapped up in something that looks like a large dead rabbit across the Scottish moors with the wind and rain lashing at his gritted teeth. He is not a natural for the savannah. He was walking by now in smaller and smaller circles and discussing less and less sensible things while glowing like a traffic light. Mark was getting red and sullen.

The two women with us thought we were complete wimps. They were Kes Hillman-Smith, a rhino expert, and Annette Lanjouw, a chimpanzee expert.

Kes Hillman-Smith took over from me on the termite hill

83
▼▼▼

and scanned the horizon. Kes is in fact one of the world's leading experts on northern white rhinos, but she was not a world authority on where in a national park the size of Scotland, the twenty-two surviving white rhino were to be at that precise moment.

I may have got my facts wrong. I seem to have conflicting information on the size of Garamba National Park. One opinion is that it is only 5,000 square kilometres, in which case I would have to say that it was only the size of part of Scotland, but it was a big enough part for twenty-two rhinoceroses to be very effectively hidden in.

Kes had been very skeptical about the termite hill from the outset, as it would befit a world expert on rhinoceroses to be, but since it had been the only thing in the distant heat haze that looked even remotely like a rhino, and we had come all this way, she had suggested that we might as well go for it.

Kes is a formidable woman, who looks as if she has just walked off the screen of a slightly naughty adventure movie: lean, fit, strikingly beautiful, and usually dressed in old combat gear that's had a number of its buttons shot off. She decided it was time to be businesslike about the map, which was a fairly rough representation of a fairly rough landscape. She worked out once and for all where the Landrover had to be, and worked it out with such ruthless determination that the Landrover would hardly dare not to be there, and eventually, of course, after miles of trekking, we discovered that it was exactly there, hiding behind a bush with a thermos of tea wedged behind the seat.

Once we had revived ourselves with the sort of mug of tea that makes the desert bloom and angels sing, we rattled and rolled our way back to our base, which was a small visitors' village of huts on the edge of Garamba National Park, separated from it by a small river. We were currently the only visitors to the park, which, as I say, is the size of part of Scotland. This is quite surprising because the park is one of

Africa's richest. It is situated in northeast Zaïre, on the border with Sudan, and takes its name from the Garamba River, which meanders from east to west through the park. Its habitat is a combination of savannah, gallery forest, and papyrus marshes, and contains currently 53,000 buffalo, 5,000 elephants, 3,000 hippos, 175 Congo giraffes, 270 species of birds, 60-odd lion, and some giant eland, which are large, spiral-horned antelopes. They know there are giant eland in the park because we saw one. The last time anybody saw one there was in the 1950s. We were rather pleased about that.

The park is very scantily visited, partly, I imagine, because of the insane bureaucratic nightmares that assail any visitor to Zaïre, but also because the park is three days' overland journey from Bunia, the nearest airport, so only the most determined visitors actually make it.

We were lucky. The Senior Management Adviser on the Garamba Rehabilitation Project, Charles Mackie, had come to pick us up from Bunia in an anti-poaching patrol Cessna 185. The runway on which we landed just outside the boundaries of the park was merely a flattened piece of grass along which we bounded and hopped before finally slowing to a halt. It was a dramatic change from the cold mistiness of the Virunga volcanoes—grassland as far as the horizon in every direction, hot, dry air, a Landrover bounding along dusty roads through the savannah, and elephants heaving themselves along in the hazy distance.

That evening we went to have a meal at the house that Kes shares with her husband, Fraser, a park conservation manager. It is a house they built themselves, out in the bush on the edge of the river, and is a long, low, rambling structure, full of books and largely open to the weather—when it rains they lower tarpaulins over the spaces where the windows aren't. For the two years it took them to build the house, they lived in a tiny mud hut with a dog, two cats, a pet

mongoose that used to dig up the floor looking for worms—
and a baby.

Because their house is so open, it is regularly full of animals. A young hippo, for instance, frequently comes to chew
on the pot plants in their living room. It often spends the
night asleep in their bedroom with its head resting next to
the (second) baby's cot. There are snakes and elephants in
the garden, rats which eat all their soap, and termites gradually nibbling away at the support poles of the house.

The only animals that really worry them are the crocodiles,
which live in the river at the bottom of the garden. Their dog
was eaten by one.

"It is a bit of a worry," Kes told us. "But we just have to
make our lives as comfortable as possible under the circum-
stances. If we lived in the city, we'd be just as concerned
about the children getting run over by a bus or abducted as
we are about them being attacked by a crocodile."

After dinner they said that if we wanted to stand a hope in
hell of actually seeing any rhino, then it would help considerably if we could find out where they actually were. They
suggested that we ask Charles to take us up in the Cessna the
next day, and then perhaps we could go out by Landrover
again the day after that and see how close we could get to
them. They contacted Charles over their battered old field
radio and made the arrangements.

Charles flies his plane the same way my mother drives her
car around the country lanes in Dorset. If you didn't know
she had done it invincibly every day of her life for years, you
would be hiding in the footwell gibbering with fear instead
of just smiling glassily and humming "Abide With Me."

Charles is a thin and slightly intense man, and also rather
shy. Sometimes you think you must have done something
that has mightily offended him, but then you realise that the
sudden silence is only because he can't think of anything to
say next and has given up. In the plane, though, there is so

much to see that he is very talkative and also, of course, very hard to hear.

He had to say it three times before I finally believed that I wasn't dreaming it—he said he just wanted to count the eggs in the nest of a saddlebilled stork at the top of the tree we were fast approaching.

He banked sharply over the top of the tree, and then appeared to put the hand brake on while he leaned out of the window and counted the eggs. The cockpit was thick with the sound of "Abide With Me" as the plane seemed slowly to start tumbling sideways out of the sky. Charles seemed to miscount twice before he was happy with the final tally, whereupon he hauled his head back through the window, turned to ask if we were doing all right, then turned back, refastened the window, and at last scooped the plane back up into the air moments before death.

From the air, the savannah looks like ostrich skin stretched across the land. We passed a small group of elephants nodding and bowing their way across the plains. Charles shouted over his shoulder at us that they have a project in Garamba National Park for training elephants, and have achieved the first major success in this field since Hannibal. African elephants are intelligent but notoriously difficult to train, and in the old Tarzan movies they used to use Indian elephants and stick bigger ears on them. The ultimate aim of this project is to use elephants on anti-poaching patrols, and also on tourist safaris. Once again, tourist revenue is seen as the one certain way of ensuring the survival of the threatened wildlife of the area.

We wheeled around in ever-increasing circles, looking out for anything resembling a rhinoceros. From up here they would clearly be much easier to distinguish from termite hills, if only for the sheer speed with which they move.

Suddenly there was one.

And there, as we passed a screen of trees, was another.

There, in fact, were another two: a mother and daughter,

87
▼▼▼

quite close to us, moving rapidly across the plain like trotting boulders. Even seen from a couple of hundred feet in the air, the sense of massive weight on the move is extraordinarily impressive. As we crossed the steady path the mother and daughter were keeping and wheeled around back over them, descending as we did so, it felt as if we were participating in a problem of three-body physics, swinging around in the gravitational pull of the rhinos.

We took another pass over them, lower and slower, directly following their path, coming as close to them as we could, and this time the sense was of taking part in military maneuvers in which we were giving air cover to some monstrous cavalry hurtling across the plain.

Shouting above the noise in the cockpit, we asked Charles if it didn't worry the rhino having us flying so close to them.

"Not half as much as it worries you," he said. "No, it doesn't bother them at all really. A rhino isn't scared of anything very much and is only really interested in what things smell like. We fly down low over them pretty regularly to get a good look at them, identify them, see what they're up to, check that they're healthy, and so on. We know them all pretty well, and we'd know if they were upset about anything."

I was struck again by something that was becoming a truism on these travels, that seeing animals such as these in a zoo was absolutely no preparation for seeing them in the wild—great beasts moving through seemingly limitless space, utterly the masters of their own world.

Or almost the masters. The next rhino we found, a mile or so farther on, was engaged in a standoff with a hyena. The hyena was circling warily around the rhino while the rhino peered at it myopically over its lowered horns. A rhino's eyesight is not particularly acute, and if it wants to get a good look at something, it will tend to look at it first with one eye and then with the other—its eyes are on either side of its skull and it can't see straight ahead. Charles pointed

out as we flew over that this rhino had had problems with hyenas before: half of its tail was missing.

By now I was beginning to feel seriously airsick and we started to head back. The purpose of the trip was just to find out where the rhinos were, and out of a total wild population of twenty-two rhinos, we had seen altogether eight. Tomorrow we would set out overland to see if we could get close to one on ground level.

One of the things that people who don't know anything about white rhinoceroses find most interesting about them is their colour.

It isn't white.

Not even remotely. It's a rather handsome dark grey. Not even a sort of pale grey that might arguably pass as an off-white, just plain dark grey. People therefore assume that zoologists are either perverse or colour-blind, but it's not that, it's that they're illiterate. "White" is a mistranslation of the Afrikaans word *weit*, meaning "wide," and it refers to the animal's mouth, which is wider than that of the black rhino. By one of those lucky chances, the white rhino is in fact a very slightly lighter shade of dark grey than the black rhino. If the white rhino had actually been darker than the black rhino, people would just get cross, which would be a pity since there are many better things to get cross about regarding the white rhino than its colour, such as what happens to its horns.

There is a widespread myth about what people want rhino horns for—in fact, two myths. The first myth is that ground rhino horn is an aphrodisiac. This, I think it's safe to say, is just what it appears to be—superstition. It has little to do with any known medical fact, and probably a lot to do with the fact that a rhino's horn is a big sticky-up hard thing.

The second myth is that anyone actually believes the first myth.

It was probably the invention of a journalist, or at best a

misunderstanding. It's easy to see where the idea came from when you consider the variety of things that the Chinese, for example, believe to be aphrodisiacs, which include the brain of a monkey, the tongue of a sparrow, the human placenta, the penis of a white horse, rabbit hair from old brushes, and the dried sexual parts of a male tiger soaked in a bottle of European brandy for six months. A big sticky-up hard thing like a rhinoceros horn would seem to be a natural for such a list, though it's perhaps harder to understand, in this context, why grinding the thing down would be such an attractive idea. The fact is that there is no actual evidence to suggest the Chinese do believe rhino horn to be an aphrodisiac. The only people who do believe it are people who've read somewhere that other people believe it, and are ready and willing to believe anything they hear that they like the sound of.

There is no known trade in rhino horn for the purposes of aphrodisia. (This, like most things, is no longer strictly true. It is now known that there are a couple of people in Northern India who use it, but they do it only to annoy.)

Some horn is used in traditional medicine in the Far East, but a major part of the trade in rhino horn is caused by something much more absurd, and it's this: fashion. Dagger handles made of rhinoceros horn are an extremely fashionable item of male jewelry in Yemen. That's it: costume jewelry.

Let's see the effect of this fashion.

Northern white rhinos were unknown to the Western world until their discovery in 1903. At the time, there were enormous numbers of them in five different countries: Chad, the Central African Republic, Sudan, Uganda, and Zaïre. But their discovery spelt disaster, because unfortunately for the northern white rhino, it has two horns—which makes it doubly attractive to poachers. The front one, the longest, averages two feet in length; the world record-holder had an incredible horn six feet long and, sadly, was worth some five thousand dollars.

By 1980, all but a thousand northern white rhinos had been killed by poachers. There were still no serious efforts to protect them and, five years later, the population reached an all-time low of just thirteen animals, all living in Garamba National Park. The animal was on the verge of extinction.

Until 1984, Garamba's 5,000 square kilometres were under the protection of a small number of staff. These staff were untrained, often unpaid, had no vehicles and no equipment. If a poacher wanted to kill a rhino, all he had to do was turn up. Even local Zaïrois occasionally killed the rhinos, to fashion small pieces of horn into rings which they believed would protect them against poison and harmful people. But most of the horn was taken by heavily armed Sudanese poachers. It was taken back to Sudan and, from there, entered the illegal international marketplace.

The situation in Garamba has improved dramatically since then, with the rehabilitation project that began in 1984. There is now a total of 246 trained staff, with eleven vehicles, a light aircraft, permanent guard posts throughout the park, and mobile patrols all in radio contact with one another. Two rhinos poached in May 1984, immediately after the rehabilitation work began, were the last to be killed in the park. The poacher was caught and imprisoned, but later allowed to escape. Attitudes have changed so much now that it is unlikely he would be allowed to escape again. Other species are still poached, but intensive protection over the past five years has at last begun to have an effect. In fact, there have been a number of rhino births and the population now stands at a slightly better twenty-two.

Twenty-two.

An astounding feature of the situation is this: the eventual value of a rhino horn, by the time it has been shipped out of Africa and fashioned into a piece of tasteless costume jewelry for some rich young Yemeni to strut around and pull girls with, is thousands of dollars. But the poacher himself, the man who goes into the park and risks his life to shoot the actual rhino that all of this time, effort, and money is going into protecting, will get about ten or twelve or fifteen dollars for the horn. So the difference between life or death for one of the rarest and most magnificent animals in the world is actually about twelve dollars.

It's easy to ask—in fact, I asked this—why not simply pay the poachers more *not* to kill the animals? The answer, of course, is very simple. If one person offers a poacher, say, twenty-five dollars not to shoot an animal, and then someone else offers him twelve dollars to shoot it, the poacher is liable to see that he can now earn thirty-seven dollars from the same animal. While the horns continue to command the amount of money they do, there is always going to be an incentive for someone to go and earn that money. So the question really is this: How do you persuade a young Yemeni that a rhino horn dagger is not a symbol of your manhood but a signal of the fact that you need such a symbol?

92
▼▼▼

Recently, there have been two separate, though unconfirmed, sightings of northern white rhinos in Southern National Park, Sudan. But the current political situation there means that very little can be done about them and, effectively, the only animals with any chance of survival have been restricted to Garamba since the mid-Eighties. They are still in a precarious position, but there is one ray of hope: experience with the southern white rhino.

Northern white rhinos and southern white rhinos belong to the same species, but their populations have been separated for such a long time that they have evolved a range of ecological and behavioural differences. More importantly, the genetic differences are so great that scientists consider them to be separate subspecies and, consequently, believe they have lived apart for more than two million years. Nowadays, they are permanently separated by a thousand miles of African rain forest, woodland, and savannah.

Without experience, the two animals are virtually impossible to tell apart, though the northern generally holds its head higher than its southern counterpart and their body proportions are also rather different.

At the time of its discovery, the northern white was by far the commoner of the two. The southern white had been discovered nearly a century earlier, but by 1882 it was considered to be extinct. Then, at the turn of the century, a small population of about eleven animals was discovered in Umfolozi, Zululand. All the stops were pulled out to save them from extinction and, by the mid-Sixties, their number had increased to about five hundred. It was enough to begin translocating individuals to other parks and reserves and to other countries. There are now more than five thousand southern white rhinos throughout southern Africa, and they are out of immediate danger.

The point is that we are not too late to save the northern white rhino from extinction.

As the sun began to go down, we went and sat by the local hippos. At a wide bend in the river the water formed a deep, slow-moving pool, and lying in the pool, grunting and bellowing, were about two hundred hippopotamuses. The opposite bank was very high, so that the pool formed a sort of natural amphitheatre for the hippos to sing in, and the sound reverberated around us with such startling clarity that I don't suppose there can be a better place in the whole of Africa for hearing a hippo grunt. The light was becoming magically warm and long, and we sat watching them for an hour, aglow with amazement. The hippos nearest to us watched with a kind of uncomprehending belligerence such as we had become used to at the airports in Zaïre, but most of them simply lay there with their heads up on their neighbours' rumps, wearing huge grins of oafish contentment. I expect I was wearing something similar myself.

Mark said that he had never seen anything like it in all his travels in Africa. Garamba, he said, was unique for the free-

dom it allowed you to get close to the animals and away from other people. There is, of course, another side to this. We heard recently that, a few weeks later, someone sitting in the exact same spot where we were sitting had been attacked and killed by a lion.

That night, as I turned in, I discovered something very interesting. When I had first checked into my hut the day before, I had noticed that the mosquito net above the bed was tied up into a huge knot. I say "noticed" in the loosest possible sense of the word. It was tied up in a knot, and when I went to bed that night, I had to untie it to drape it over the bed. Further than that, I had paid no attention to it whatsoever.

Tonight, I discovered why it is that mosquito nets get tied up into knots. The reason is embarrassingly simple, and I can hardly bear to admit what it is. It's to stop the mosquitoes from getting into it.

I climbed into bed and gradually realised that there were almost as many mosquitoes inside the net as outside. The action of draping the net over myself was almost as much use as the magnificent fence that the Australians built across the whole of their continent to keep the rabbits out when there were already rabbits on both sides of the fence. Nervously I shone my torch up into the dome of the net. It was black with mozzies.

I tried to brush them out, and lost a few of them. I unhooked the net from the ceiling and flapped it vigorously around the room. That woke them up and got them interested. I turned the thing completely inside out, took it outside and flapped it about a lot more till it seemed that I had got rid of most of them, took it back into the room, hung it up, and climbed into bed. Almost immediately I was being bitten crazy. I shone my torch up into the dome. It was still black with mozzies. I took the net down again, laid it out on the floor, and tried to scrape the mosquitoes off with the edge of my portable computer, which the batteries had fallen out of, thus making it useful for little else. Didn't work. I tried it again with the edge of my writing pad. That was a bit more effective, but it meant that I was trying to write between dozens of smeared mosquito corpses for the next few days. I hung the net up again and went to bed. It was still full of mosquitoes, all of which were now in a vigorous biting mood. They buzzed and zizzed around me in an excited rage.

Right.

I took the net down. I laid it on the floor and I jumped on it. I continued jumping on it for a good ten minutes, till I was certain that every square centimetre of the thing had been jumped on at least six times, and then I jumped on it some more. Then I found a book and smacked it with the book all over. Then I jumped on it some more, smacked it with the book again, took it outside, shook it out, took it back in, hung it up, and climbed into bed underneath it. The net was full of very angry mosquitoes. It was by now about four in the morning, and by the time Mark came to wake me at about six to go looking for rhinoceroses, I was not in the mood for wildlife, and said so. He laughed in his cheery kind of way and offered me half of a tinned sausage for breakfast. I took that and a mug of powdered coffee, and walked down to the riverbank, which was about fifty yards away. I stood ankle deep in the cool, quietly flowing water, listening to the early-morning noises of the birds and insects, and biting the sausage, and after a while began to be revived by the dawning realisation of how absurd I must look.

Charles arrived in the Landrover along with Annette Lanjouw and we piled our stuff for the day into it and set off.

As we bumped and rattled our way out into the savannah once more, deep into the area where we had seen the rhino the previous day from the plane, I asked in a very casual, matter-of-fact, just-out-of-interest kind of way whether or not rhino were actually dangerous.

Mark grinned and shook his head. He said we'd be very unlucky indeed to be hurt by a rhino. This didn't seem to me

entirely to answer the question, but I didn't like to press the point. I was only asking out of mild curiosity.

Mark went on anyway.

"You hear a lot of stuff that simply isn't true," he said, "or at least is blown up out of all proportion, just because it sounds dramatic. It really irritates me when people pretend that animals they meet are dangerous, just so it makes them seem brave or intrepid. It's like fishermen's tales. A lot of early explorers were really terrible exaggerators. They would double or quadruple the length of the snakes they saw. Perfectly innocent anacondas became sixty-foot monsters that lay in wait to crush people to death. All complete rubbish. But the anaconda's reputation has been damaged for good."

"But rhinos are perfectly safe?"

"Oh, more or less. I'd be a bit wary of black rhinos if I was on foot. They have got a reputation for unprovoked aggression which I suppose they've pretty much earned themselves. One black rhino in Kenya caught me off guard once, and severely dented a friend's car, which I'd borrowed for the day. He'd only had it a few weeks. His previous car, which I had borrowed for the weekend, had been written off by a buffalo. It was all very embarrassing. Hello, have we found something."

Charles had brought the Landrover to a halt and was peering at the horizon through his binoculars.

"Okay," he said. "I think I can see one. About two miles away."

We each looked through our own binoculars, following his directions. The early-morning air was still cool, and there was no heat haze frying the horizon. Once I had worked out which group of trees in front of a tussocky hill it was we were meant to be looking just to the left and slightly in front of, I eventually found myself looking at something that looked suspiciously like the termite hill we had almost killed ourselves tracking down two days earlier. It was very still.

"Sure it's a rhino?" I asked politely.

"Yup," said Charles. "Dead sure. We'll stay parked here. They have very keen hearing and the noise of the Landrover would send it away if we drove any closer. So we walk."

We gathered our cameras together and walked.

"Quietly," said Charles.

We walked more quietly.

It was difficult to be that quiet struggling through a wide, marsh-filled gully, with our boots and even our knees farting and belching in the mud. Mark entertained us by whispering interesting facts to us.

"Did you know," he said, "that bilharzia is the second most common disease in the world after tooth decay?"

"No, really," I said.

"It's very interesting," said Mark. "It's a disease you get from wading through infected water. Tiny snails breed in the water and they act as hosts to tiny parasitic worms that latch on to your skin. When the water evaporates, the worms burrow in and attack your bladder and intestines. You'll know if you've got it, because it's like really bad flu with diarrhea, and you also piss blood."

"I think we're meant to be keeping quiet," I said.

Once we were on the other side of the gully, we regrouped again behind some trees and Charles checked on the wind direction and gave us some further instructions.

"You need to know something about the way that a rhino sees his world before we go barging into it," he whispered to us. "They're pretty mild and inoffensive creatures for all their size and horns and everything. His eyesight is very poor and he only relies on it for pretty basic information. If he sees five animals like us approaching him, he'll get nervous and run off. So we have to keep close together in single file. Then he'll think we're just one animal and he'll be less worried."

"A pretty big animal," I said.

"That doesn't matter. He's not afraid of big animals, but numbers bother him. We also have to stay downwind of him, which means that from here we're going to have to make a

97
▼▼▼

wide circle around him. His sense of smell is very acute indeed. In fact, it's his most important sense. His whole world picture is made up of smells. He 'sees' in smells. His nasal passages are in fact bigger than his brain.''

From here it was at last possible to discern the creature with the naked eye. We were a bit more than half a mile from it. It was standing out in the open, looking, at moments when it was completely still, like a large outcrop of rock. From time to time its long sloping head would wave gently from side to side and its horns would bob slightly up and down as, mildly and inoffensively, it cropped the grass. This was not a termite hill.

We set off again, very quietly, constantly stopping, ducking, and shifting our position to try and stay downwind of the creature, while the wind, which didn't care one way or the other, constantly shifted its position too. At last we made it to another small clump of trees about a hundred yards from the creature, which so far had seemed to be undisturbed by our approach. From here, though it was just open ground between us and it. We stayed here for a few minutes to watch and photograph it. If any closer approach did in fact scare it off, then this was our last opportunity. The animal was turned slightly away from us, continuing gently to crop the grass. At last the wind was well established in our favour and, nervously, quietly, we set off again.

It was a little like that game we play as children, in which one child stands facing the wall while the others try to creep up behind and touch her. She will from time to time suddenly turn around, and anyone she catches moving has to go all the way to the back and start again. Generally she won't be in a position to impale anyone she doesn't like the look of on a three-foot-horn, but in other respects it was similar.

The animal is, of course, a herbivore. It lives by grazing. The closer we crept to it, and the more monstrously it loomed in front of us, the more incongruous its gentle activity seemed to be. It was like watching an excavating machine quietly getting on with a little weeding.

At about forty yards' distance, the rhinoceros suddenly stopped eating and looked up. It turned slowly to look at us and regarded us with grave suspicion while we tried very hard to look like the smallest and most inoffensive animal we could possibly be. It watched us carefully but without apparent comprehension, its small black eyes peering dully at us from either side of its horn. You can't help but try and follow an animal's thought processes, and you can't help, when faced with an animal like a three-ton rhinoceros with nasal passages bigger than its brain, but fail.

The world of smells is now virtually closed to modern man. Not that we haven't got a sense of smell—we sniff our food or wine, we occasionally smell a flower, and can usually tell if there's a gas leak—but generally it's all a bit of a blur, and often an irrelevant or bothersome blur at that. When we read that Napoleon wrote to Josephine on one occasion, "Don't wash—I'm coming home," we are simply bemused and almost think of it as a deviant behaviour. We are so used to thinking of sight, closely followed by hearing, as the chief of the senses that we find it hard to visualise (the word itself is a giveaway) a world that declares itself primarily to the sense of smell. Its not a world our mental processors can resolve—or, at least, they are no longer practiced in resolving it. For a great many animals, however, smell is the chief of the senses. It tells them what is good to eat and what is not (we go by what the packet tells us and the sell-by date). It guides them toward food that isn't within line of sight (we already know where the shops are). It works at night (we turn on the light). It tells them of the presence and state of mind of other animals (we use language). It also tells them what other animals have been in the vicinity and doing what in the last day or two (we simply don't know, unless they've left a note). Rhinoceroses declare their movements and their

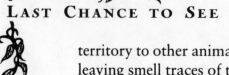

territory to other animals by stamping in their feces, and then leaving smell traces of themselves wherever they walk, which is the sort of note we would not appreciate being left.

When we smell something slightly unexpected, if we can't immediately make sense of it and it isn't particularly bothersome, we simply ignore it, and this is probably equivalent to the rhino's reaction to seeing us. It appeared not to make any particular decision about us, but merely to forget that it had a decision to make. The grass presented it with something infinitely richer and more interesting to its senses, and the animal returned to cropping it.

We crept on closer. Eventually we got to within about twenty-five yards, and Charles signaled us to stop. We were close enough. Quite close enough. We were in fact astoundingly close to it.

The animal measured about six feet high at its shoulders, and sloped down gradually toward its hindquarters and its rear legs, which were chubby with muscle. The sheer immensity of every part of it exercised a fearful magnetism on the mind. When the rhino moved a leg, just slightly, huge muscles moved easily under its heavy skin like Volkswagens parking.

The noise of our cameras seemed to distract it and it looked up again, but not in our direction. It appeared not to know what to think about this, and after a while returned to its grazing.

The light breeze that was blowing toward us began to shift its direction, and we shifted with it, which brought us around more to the front of the rhino. This seemed to us, in our world dominated by vision, to be an odd thing to do, but so long as the rhino could not smell us, it could take or leave what we looked like. It then turned slightly toward us itself, so that we were suddenly crouched in full view of the beast. It seemed to chew a little more thoughtfully, but for a while paid us no more mind than that. We watched quietly for fully three or four minutes, and even the sound of our cameras ceased to bother the animal. After a few minutes we became a little more careless about noise, and started to talk to one another about our reactions, and now the rhino became a little more restive and uneasy. It stopped grazing, lifted its head, and looked at us steadily for about a minute, still uncertain what to do.

Again, I imagine myself sitting here in my study writing this through the afternoon and gradually realising that a slight smell I had noticed earlier is still there, and beginning to wonder if I should start to look for other clues as to what it could be. I would start to *look* for something, something I could see: a bottle of something that's fallen over, or something electrical that's overheating. The smell is simply the clue that there's something I should look for.

For the rhino, the sight of us was simply a clue that there was something he should sniff for, and he began to sniff the air more carefully, and to move around in a slow, careful arc. At that moment the wind began to move around and gave us away completely. The rhino snapped to attention, turned away from us, and hurtled off across the plain like a nimble young tank.

We had seen our northern white rhinoceros, and it was time to go home.

The next day, Charles flew us back across the ostrich-skin savannah to Bunia airport, where we were due once more to pick up a missionary flight returning to Nairobi. The plane was already there waiting and a representative from the airline assured us, against the evidence of all our previous experience, that there would be no problems, we could go straight to the plane. Then, a few minutes later, we were told that we would just have to go quickly to the immigration office. We could leave our bags. We went to the immigration office, where we were told that we should bring our bags. We brought our bags. Expensive-looking camera equipment.

We were then confronted by a large Zaïrois official in a

101
▼▼▼

natty blue suit whom we had noticed earlier hanging around watching us take our baggage out of Charles's plane. I had had the feeling then that he was sizing us up for something.

He examined our passports for a good long time before acknowledging our presence at all, then at last he looked up at us, and a wide smile crept slowly across his face.

"You entered the country," he asked, "at Bukavu?"

In fact, he said it in French, so we made a bit of a meal of understanding him, which was something that experience had taught us to do. Eventually we admitted that, insofar as we had understood the question, yes, we had entered at Bukavu.

"Then," he said quietly, triumphantly, "you must leave from Bukavu."

He made no move to give us back our passports.

We looked at him blankly.

He explained slowly. Tourists, he said, had to leave the country from the same port by which they had entered. Smile.

102
▼▼▼

We utterly failed to understand what he had said. This was almost true, anyway. It was the most preposterous invention. He still held on to our passports. Next to him a young girl was sitting, studiously copying down copious information from other visitors' passports, information that would almost certainly never see the light of day again.

We stood and argued while our plane sat out on the tarmac waiting to take off to Nairobi, but the official simply sat and held our passports. We knew it was nonsense. He knew we knew it was nonsense. That was clearly part of the pleasure of it. He smiled at us again, gave us a slow contented shrug, and idly brushed a bit of fluff off the sleeve of the natty blue suit toward the cost of which he clearly expected a major contribution.

On the wall above him, gazing seriously into the middle distance from a battered frame, stood the figure of President Mobutu, resplendent in his leopard-skin pillbox hat.

HEARTBEATS
IN THE NIGHT

I F YOU TOOK THE whole of Norway, scrunched it up a bit, shook out all the moose and reindeer, hurled it ten thousand miles around the world, and filled it with birds, then you'd be wasting your time, because it looks very much as if someone has already done it.

Fiordland, a vast tract of mountainous terrain that occupies the southwest corner of South Island, New Zealand, is one of the most astounding pieces of land anywhere on God's earth, and one's first impulse, standing on a clifftop surveying it all, is simply to burst into spontaneous applause.

It is magnificent. It is awe-inspiring. The land is folded and twisted and broken on such a scale that it makes your brain quiver and sing in your skull just trying to comprehend what it is looking at. Mountains and clouds jumbled on top of

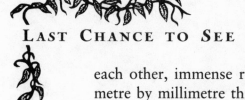

each other, immense rivers of ice cracking their way millimetre by millimetre through the ravines, cataracts thundering down into the narrow green valleys below—it all shines so luminously in the magically clear light of New Zealand that to eyes which are accustomed to the grimier air of most of the Western world, it seems too vivid to be real.

When Captain Cook saw it from the sea in 1773, he recorded that "inland as far as the eye can see the peaks are crowded together as to scarcely admit any valleys between them." The great forked valleys have been carved out by glaciers over millions of years, and many are flooded by the sea for many miles inland. Some of the cliff faces drop hundreds of feet sheer into the water, and continue sheer for hundreds of feet below it. It still has the appearance of a work in progress. Despite relentless lashing by the wind and rain, it is sharp and jagged in its immensity.

Much of it has still not been explored at ground level. The only roads that approach the Fiordland National Park peter out quickly in the foothills, and most visiting tourists only ever explore the fringe scenery. A few backpackers plunge further in, and very, very few experienced campers try to get anywhere near the heart of it. Looking out across its serrated masses and its impossibly deep ravines, you feel that the very idea of trying to cross it on foot is ludicrous. Most serious exploration is of small local pockets, reached by helicopter, which is how we came to it.

Bill Black is said to be one of the most experienced helicopter pilots in the world, and he needs to be. He sits like a cuddly old curmudgeon hunched over his joystick and chews gum slowly and continuously as he flies his helicopter directly at sheer cliff faces to see if you'll scream. Just as the helicopter seems about to smash itself against the rock wall, an updraught catches it and wafts it impossibly up and over the top of the ridge, which then falls away again precipitously on the other side, leaving us swinging out over a void. The valley lurches sickeningly away beneath us and we drop down a few feet, twisting to face up the next ravine as we do so, as if we are being swung by a giant on the end of an immense rubber rope.

The helicopter puts its nose down and goes thrumming its way along the ravine wall. We startle a couple of birds that scatter up into the air way ahead of us, flying with fast, sharp wing beats. Mark quickly scrabbles under his seat for his binoculars.

"Keas!" he says. I nod but only very slightly. My head already has quite enough contrary motions to contend with.

"They're mountain parrots," says Mark. "Very intelligent birds with long curved beaks. They can rip the windscreen wipers off cars and often do."

I'm always startled by the speed with which Mark is able to recognise birds he's never seen before, even when they're just a speck in the distance.

"The wing beat is very distinctive," he explains. "But it would be even easier to identify them if we weren't in a helicopter with all this noise. It's one of those birds which very helpfully calls out its own name when it's flying. 'Kea! Kea! Kea!' Birdwatchers love them for that. It would be great if the Pallas's grasshopper warbler would learn the same trick. Make warbler identification a lot easier." He follows them for a few seconds more, until they round a large out-crop and disappear from view. He puts down his binoculars. They are not what we have come to look for.

"Interesting birds, though, with some odd habits. Very fussy about getting the design of their nests right. There was one kea nest that was found which the birds had started to build in 1958. In 1965 they were still sorting it out and adding bits to it but hadn't actually moved in yet. Bit like you in that respect."

As we reach the narrow end of the ravine, we pause briefly a few yards from a cataract crashing down its sides to fill the river hundreds of feet beneath us. We peer out at it from our floating glass bubble and I feel suddenly like a visitor from

105
▼▼▼

another planet, descending from the sky to study the minutiae of an alien world. I also feel sick but decide to keep this information to myself.

With a slight shrug, Bill heaves the helicopter way up out of the ravine and into the clear air again. The sheer immensity of the volumes of rock and space that turn easily around us continually overwhelms the spatial processors of the brain. And then, just when you think that you have experienced all the wonders that this world has to offer, you round a peak and suddenly think you're doing the whole thing over again, but this time on drugs.

We are skimming over the tops of glaciers. The sudden splurge of light blinds us for a moment, but when the light coalesces into solid shapes, they are like shapes from dreams. Great top-heavy towers resembling the deformed torsos of giants; huge sculpted caves and arches; and here and there the cracked and splayed remains of what looks like a number of Gothic cathedrals dropped from a considerable height: but all is snow and ice. It's as if the ghosts of Salvador Dalí and Henry Moore come here at night with the elements and play.

106
▼▼▼

I have the instinctive reaction of Western man when confronted with the sublimely incomprehensible: I grab my camera and start to photograph it. I feel I'll be able to cope with it all more easily when it's just two square inches of colour on a light box and my chair isn't trying to throw me around the room.

Gaynor, our radio producer, thrusts a microphone at me and asks me to describe what we're looking at.

"What?" I say, and gibber slightly.

"More," she says, "more!"

I gibber some more. The blades of the helicopter rotor are spinning mere inches from a tower of ice.

She sighs. "Well, it will probably edit up into something," she says and turns the tape off again.

We take one more mind-wrenching turn around the giant

ice sculptures and then head off down the ravines once more, which now seem almost domestic by comparison.

There is one other passenger in the aircraft: Don Merton, a benign man with the air of a vicar apologising for something. He sits quietly, occasionally pushing his spectacles back up the bridge of his nose and murmuring, "Yes, ah yes," to himself, as if this all confirmed something he'd always rather suspected. In fact, he knows the area very well. He works for the New Zealand Department of Conservation and has probably done more than any man living to preserve the threatened birds of New Zealand.

We are once again very close to the rock wall of the ravine, with hundreds of feet of sheer drop beneath us, and I notice that we are following a long narrow path that runs along an impossibly narrow ledge inclining gradually upward toward a spur overlooking a broader sweep of valley. I suffer from terrible vertigo. Being six foot five means I sometimes get giddy just standing up, and the very sight of the path gives me black swimmy nightmares.

"We used to come up that quite a lot," murmurs Don, leaning forward to point at it.

I look at him in astonishment and then back at the terrifying path. We are hovering now just feet from it and the dull thudding of the rotor blades is reverberating back at us. The pathway is just a foot or two wide, grassy and slippery.

"Yes, I suppose it is a bit steep," says Don with a gentle laugh, as if that was the only reason they didn't do it by bicycle. "There's a track and bowl system up on top of that ridge ahead of us. Want to take a look?"

We nod nervously and Bill flies on.

I had often heard the term *track and bowl system* bandied about by New Zealand zoologists, and they had bandied it about so casually that I hadn't wanted to say that I hadn't the faintest idea what they were talking about. I decided to start from the premise that it had something to do with satellite dishes and work it out gradually from there. This led to my being in a state of complete incomprehension for about two days before I finally plucked up the courage to admit my ignorance.

A track and bowl system is nothing whatever to do with satellite dishes. It does, however, share with them this feature —that it is likely to be found in high, open places. It's a rather odd name for an extremely odd phenomenon. A track and bowl system doesn't look particularly dramatic, and indeed if you were not a New Zealand zoologist, you might pass one by without even noticing it, but it is the site of one of the most peculiar pieces of behaviour performed by any animal on earth.

The helicopter sweeps out beyond the ridge into the open valley, turns and approaches the ridge again from the other side, lifts on the updraught, turns slightly again—and settles. We have landed.

We sit in stunned silence for a moment, scarcely believing what we have just landed on. The ridge is only a few yards wide. It plunges for hundreds of feet on either side, and falls away rapidly in front of us as well.

Bill turns and grins at us. "No worries," he says, which I thought they only said in Australia. This is the kind of thought you need to distract you at moments like this.

Nervously we climb out and, tucking our heads under the turning blades, scramble out onto the ridge. Spread out around our promontory is a deep, jagged valley plunging away from us on three sides, softening in its contours at its lower levels. Just beyond us it makes a sharp left turn and proceeds by a series of sharp twists and folds to the Tasman Sea, which is a hazy glimmer in the far distance. The few clouds, which are not that far above us, trace the undulations of the valley with their crisp shadows as they make their way slowly along it, and this alone gives us a clear sense of scale and perspective.

When the thudding blades of the helicopter are finally still, the spacious murmur of the valley gradually rises to fill the silence: the low thunder of cataracts, the distant hiss of the sea, the rustling of the breeze in the scrubby grass, the keas explaining who they are to one another. There is one sound, however, that we know we are not going to hear—not just because we have arrived at the wrong time of day, but because we have arrived in the wrong year. There will not be any more right years.

Until 1987 Fiordland was the home of one of the strangest, most unearthly sounds in the world. For thousands of years, in the right season, the sound could be heard after nightfall throughout these wild peaks and valleys.

It was like a heartbeat: a deep, powerful throb that echoed through the dark ravines. It was so deep that some people will tell you that they felt it stirring in their gut before they could discern the actual sound, a sort of *wump,* a heavy wobble of air. Most people have never heard it at all, or ever will again. It was the sound of the kakapo, the old night parrot of New Zealand, sitting high on a rocky promontory and calling for a mate.

Of all the creatures we were searching for this year, it was probably the strangest and most intriguing, and also one of the rarest and most difficult to find. Once, before New Zealand was inhabited by humans, there were hundreds of thousands of kakapos. Then there were thousands, then hundreds. Then there were just forty . . . and counting. Here in Fiordland, which for many thousands of years was the bird's main stronghold, there are now thought to be none left at all.

Don Merton knows more about these birds than anyone else in the world, and he has come along with us partly as our guide, but also because this flight into Fiordland gives him the opportunity to check one last time: has the last kakapo definitely gone?

Our helicopter is perched at such a dizzying angle on the high ridge of rock, it looks as if the merest puff of wind will

toss it lightly away into the valley far below us. Mark and I walk slowly away from it with a stiff, uneasy gait as if we are aching all over. Any move we make we make first with our heads before daring to move the rest of our bodies. Bill Black grins at us wickedly for being earthbound city boys.

"No worries," he says cheerfully. "Wherever we can land, we put down. This is where Don wanted to come, so this is where I put him. Wouldn't want to be here if there was a high wind blowing, but there isn't." He sits on a small rock and lights a cigarette. "Not right now, anyhow," he adds and peers off into the distance, happily contemplating the enormous fun we would all have if a gale suddenly whipped up along the valley.

Gaynor feels disinclined, for the moment, to move too far away from the chopper, and decides that this might be a good moment to interview Bill. She pulls the tangled coloured cables of the cassette recorder out of her shoulder bag and jams the tiny headphones over her hair, without ever looking down to the left or the right. She thrusts the microphone at him and uses her other hand to steady herself nervously against the ground.

"I've been flying in Fiordland for fifteen years," says Bill, when she's ready, "mostly telecommunications work, and some construction work. Don't do tourists usually. Can't be bothered with that. Otherwise I do a lot of work for the kakapo transfer program, flying the wardens around to the most inaccessible parts of New Zealand. A helicopter's very useful for that, because it can put down in the most unlikely places. You see that rocky peak over there?"

"No!" says Gaynor, still staring fixedly at the ground. "I don't want to look yet. Just . . . tell me a story. Tell me . . . tell me something funny that's happened to you. Please?"

"Something funny, eh?" says Bill and takes a long, thoughtful drag on his cigarette as he surveys the valley. "Well, I once set my hands on fire in the helicopter, because

I lit a match without realising my gloves were soaked in petrol. That the sort of thing you had in mind?"

Don Merton, in the meantime, has calmly walked off a few yards, and is peering anxiously at a patch of the scrubby ground. He squats down and very carefully brushes aside pieces of loose earth and grass from a shallow depression in the earth. He finds something and picks it up. It is small, roughly oval in shape, and pale in colour. He examines it carefully for a while and his shoulders sag dejectedly. He beckons us over to join him. We follow nervously and look at the thing he is holding up between his fingers and regarding with extraordinary sadness. It is a single, slightly elderly, sweet potato. I hardly know what to say.

With a sigh he replaces the sweet potato on the ground.

"We call this place Kakapo Castle," he says, looking up and squinting at us in the cold, bright sunlight. "It is the last known kakapo booming site in the whole of mainland New Zealand. This shallow pit in the earth here is part of a track and bowl system."

I'll explain what a track and bowl system actually is in a moment. All there is to see here is the roughly dug shallow pit in the ground. It's untidy and a little overgrown. Looking around again at the breathtaking landscape spread out around us, I feel bewildered. We have flown so far into this shattering immensity of land, and all to find these small sad scrapings in the earth and no egg, just a potato.

I make some lame remark along these lines. Mark frowns at me and a cloudy look comes over Don's face.

"Oh no," says Don, "I wasn't expecting an egg. Not an egg. Not here. Oh no, not at all."

"Oh," I say, "I thought when you picked up the potato . . ."

Mark says out of the corner of his mouth, "Don explained all this in the helicopter."

"I couldn't hear anything in the helicopter."

"You won't find eggs in a track and bowl system, you see," says Don patiently. "It's just the courtship and mating area. I put the sweet potato there myself when I last came up here, last year. If there was a kakapo in the area, it would have eaten the potato." He picks it up again and hands it to me.

"There, you see? Not a mark on it. Not a nibble. And it would have trimmed and tidied its booming bowl. They are very meticulous birds. We don't know what's happened to the last one here. It may have been killed, possibly by a cat. We think they sometimes can come up this high. Fiordland is full of cats, which is bad news for the kakapo. Though probably not all cats would have a go at a kakapo. Some will have tried—and failed—to savage a kiwi and might therefore steer clear of kakapos. Others might have tried it, found they could get away with it, and done it again. Kakapos are generally unused to defending themselves. They'll just freeze if they see a cat approach. Though they have powerful legs and claws, they don't use them for defence. A kiwi, on the other hand, will kick hell out of a cat. Because kiwi fight each other. Put two in a cage together and there'll be a dead one in the morning.

"Or the kakapo may simply have died of old age. We don't know how long they live, though it seems that it might be a long time. Maybe as long as humans. Either way, the kakapo's not here anymore, I think we can be quite sure of that. There are now no kakapos left in all of Fiordland."

He takes the potato back from me, nevertheless, and with a last gesture of hopeless optimism puts it carefully back on the edge of the bowl.

Until relatively recently—in the evolutionary scale of things —the wildlife of New Zealand consisted of almost nothing but birds. Only birds could reach the place. The ancestors of many of the birds that are now natives of New Zealand originally flew there. There was also a couple of species of bats, which are mammals, but—and this is the point—there

112
▼▼▼

were no predators. No dogs, no cats, no ferrets or weasels, nothing that the birds needed to escape from particularly.

And flight, of course, is a means of escape. It's a survival mechanism, and one that the birds of New Zealand found they didn't especially need. Flying is hard work and consumes a lot of energy.

Not only that. There is also a trade-off between flying and eating. The more you eat, the harder it is to fly. So increasingly what happened was that instead of having just a light snack and then flying off, the birds would settle in for a rather larger meal and go for a waddle afterward instead.

So when eventually European settlers arrived and brought cats and dogs and stoats and possums with them, a lot of New Zealand's flightless birds were suddenly waddling for their lives. The kiwis, the takahes—and the old night parrots, the kakapos.

Of these, the kakapo is the strangest. Well, I suppose the penguin is a pretty peculiar kind of creature when you think about it, but it's quite a robust kind of peculiarness, and the bird is perfectly well adapted to the world in which it finds itself, in a way that the kakapo is not. The kakapo is a bird out of time. If you look one in its large, round, greeny-brown face, it has a look of serenely innocent incomprehension that makes you want to hug it and tell it that everything will be all right, though you know that it probably will not be.

It is an extremely fat bird. A good-sized adult will weigh about six or seven pounds, and its wings are just about good for waggling a bit if it thinks it's about to trip over something —but flying is completely out of the question. Sadly, however, it seems that not only has the kakapo forgotten how to fly, but it has also forgotten that it has forgotten how to fly. Apparently a seriously worried kakapo will sometimes run up a tree and jump out of it, whereupon it flies like a brick and lands in a graceless heap on the ground.

By and large, though, the kakapo has never learned to worry. It's never had anything much to worry about.

Most birds, faced with a predator, will at least realise that something's up and make a bolt for safety, even if it means abandoning any eggs or chicks in its nest. But not the kakapo. Its reaction when confronted with a predator is that it simply doesn't know what the form is. It has no conception of the idea that anything could possibly want to hurt it, so it tends just to sit on its nest in a state of complete confusion and leaves the other animal to make the next move—which is usually a fairly swift and final one.

It's frustrating to think of the difference that language would make. The millennia crawl by pretty bloody slowly while natural selection sifts its way obliviously through generation after generation, favouring the odd aberrant kakapo, which is a little twitchier than its contemporaries, till the species as a whole finally gets the idea. It would all be cut short in a moment if one of them could say, "When you see one of those things with whiskers and little bitey teeth, run like hell." On the other hand, human beings, who are almost unique in having the ability to learn from the experience of others, are also remarkable for their apparent disinclination to do so.

The trouble is that this predator business has all happened rather suddenly in New Zealand, and by the time nature starts to select in favour of slightly more nervous and fleet-footed kakapos, there won't be any left at all, unless deliberate human intervention can protect them from what they can't deal with themselves. It would help if there were plenty of them being born, but this brings us on to more problems. The kakapo is a solitary creature: it doesn't like other animals. It doesn't even like the company of other kakapos. One conservation worker we met said he sometimes wondered if the mating call of the male didn't actively repel the female, which is the sort of biological absurdity you otherwise find only in discotheques. The ways in which the kakapo goes about mating are wonderfully bizarre, extraordinarily long drawn out, and almost totally ineffective.

Here's what they do.

The male kakapo builds himself a track and bowl system, which is simply a roughly dug shallow depression in the earth, with one or two pathways leading through the undergrowth toward it. The only thing that distinguishes the tracks from those that would be made by any other animal blundering its way about is that the vegetation on either side of them is rather precisely clipped.

The kakapo is looking for good acoustics when he does this, so the track and bowl system will often be sited against a rock facing out across a valley, and when the mating season arrives, he sits in his bowl and booms.

This is an extraordinary performance. He puffs out two enormous air sacs on either side of his chest, sinks his head down into them, and starts to make what he feels are sexy grunting noises. These noises gradually descend in pitch, resonate in his two air sacs, and reverberate through the night air, filling the valleys for miles around with the eerie sound of an immense heart beating in the night.

The booming noise is deep, very deep, just on the threshold of what you can actually hear and what you can feel. This means that it carries for very great distances, but that you can't tell where it's coming from. If you're familiar with certain types of stereo setups, you'll know that you can get an additional speaker called a sub-woofer which carries only the bass frequencies and which you can, in theory, stick anywhere in the room, even behind the sofa. The principle is the same: you can't tell where the bass sound is coming from.

The female kakapo can't tell where the booming is coming from either, which is something of a shortcoming in a mating call. "Come and *get* me!" "Where are you?" "Come and *get* me!" "Where the hell are you?" "Come and *get* me!" "Look, do you want me to come or not?" "Come and *get* me!" "Oh, for heaven's sake." "Come and *get* me!" "Go and stuff yourself," is roughly how it would go in human terms.

115
▼▼▼

As it happens, the male has a wide variety of other noises it can make as well, but we don't know what they're all for. Well, I only know what I'm told, of course, but zoologists who've studied the bird for years say they don't know what it's all in aid of. The noises include a high-frequency, metallic, nasal "ching" noise, humming, bill-clicking, "scrarking" (scrarking is simply what it sounds like—the bird goes "scrark" a lot), "screech-crowing," piglike grunts and squeals, ducklike "warks," and donkeylike braying. There are also the distress calls that the young make when they trip over something or fall out of trees, and these make up yet another wide range of long-drawn-out, vibrant, complaining croaks.

I've heard a tape of collected kakapo noises, and it's almost impossible to believe that it all comes just from a bird, or indeed any kind of animal. Pink Floyd studio outtakes perhaps, but not a parrot.

Some of these other noises get heard in the later stages of courtship. The chinging, for instance, which doesn't carry so well, is very directional and can help any females that have been aroused by night after night of booming (it sometimes goes on for seven hours a night for up to three months) to find a mate. This doesn't always work, though. Females in breeding condition have been known to turn up at completely unoccupied bowls, wait around for a while, and then go away again.

It's not that they're not willing. When they are in breeding condition, their sex drive is extremely strong. One female kakapo is known to have walked twenty miles in one night to visit a mate, and then walked home again in the morning. Unfortunately, however, the period during which the female is prepared to behave like this is rather short. As if things aren't difficult enough already, the female can only come into breeding condition when a particular plant, the podocarp for instance, is bearing fruit. This only happens every two years. Until it does, the male can boom all he likes, it won't do him any good. The kakapo's pernickety dietary requirements are a whole other area of exasperating difficulty. It makes me tired just to think of them, so I think we'll pass quickly over all that. Imagine being an airline steward trying to serve meals to a plane full of Moslems, Jews, vegetarians, vegans, and diabetics when all you've got is turkey because it's Christmastime, and that will give you the idea.

The males therefore get extremely overwrought sitting in their bowls making noises for months on end, waiting for their mates, who are waiting for a particular type of tree to fruit. When one of the rangers who was working in an area where kakapos were booming happened to leave his hat on the ground, he came back later to find a kakapo attempting to ravish it. On another occasion the discovery of some ruffled possum fur in the mating area suggested that a kakapo had made another alarming mistake, an experience which is unlikely to have been satisfying to either party.

The net result of all these months of excavating and booming and walking and scrarking and being fussy about fruit is that once every three or four years the female kakapo lays one single egg which promptly gets eaten by a stoat.

So the big question is: How on earth has the kakapo managed to last *this* long?

Speaking as a non-zoologist confronted with this bird, I couldn't help but wonder if nature, freed from the constraints of having to produce something that would survive a great deal of competition, wasn't simply making it up as it went along. Doodling in fact. "How about sticking this bit in? Can't do any harm, might be quite entertaining."

In fact, the kakapo is a bird that in some ways reminds me of the British motorbike industry. It had things its own way for so long that it simply became eccentric. The motorbike industry didn't respond to market forces because it wasn't particularly aware of them. It built a certain number of motorbikes and a certain number of people bought them and that was that. It didn't seem to matter much that they were

noisy, complicated to maintain, sprayed oil all over the place, and had their own very special way, as T. E. Lawrence discovered at the end of his life, of going around corners. That was what motorbikes did, and if you wanted a motorbike, that was what you got. End of story. And, of course, it very nearly was the end of the story for the British industry when the Japanese suddenly got the idea that motorbikes didn't have to be that way. They could be sleek, they could be clean, they could be reliable and well-behaved. Maybe then a whole new world of people would buy them, not just those whose idea of fun was spending Sunday afternoon in the shed with an oily rag, or marching on 'Aqaba.

These highly competitive machines arrived in the British Isles (again, it's island species that have never learned to compete hard. I know that Japan is a bunch of islands too, but for the purposes of this analogy, I'm cheerfully going to ignore the fact) and British motorbikes almost died out overnight.

Almost, but not quite. They were kept alive by a bunch of enthusiasts who felt that though the Nortons and Triumphs might be difficult and curmudgeonly beasts, they had guts and immense character and the world would be a much poorer place without them. They have been through a lot of difficult changes in the last decade or so, but have now re-emerged, reengineered as highly prized, bike-lovers' bikes. I think this analogy is now in serious danger of breaking down, so perhaps I had better abandon it.

A few days earlier than all this, before we ventured out into Fiordland, I had had a dream.

I dreamt that I awoke to find myself lying on a remote beach spread-eagled on huge, round, pink and pale blue boulders and unable to move, my head filled with the slow roar of the sea. I awoke from this dream to find myself lying spread-eagled on huge, round, pink and pale blue boulders on a beach and dazed with confusion. I couldn't move because my camera bag was slung around my neck and jammed behind a boulder.

I struggled to my feet and looked out to sea, trying to work out where on earth I was and if I was still embroiled in a recursion of dreams. Perhaps I was still on a plane going somewhere and was just watching an inflight movie. I looked around for a stewardess, but there was no one coming along the beach with a tray of drinks. I looked down at my boots and that seemed to trigger something in my head. The last clear memory that came to mind of looking closely at my boots was after emerging from a bog in Zaïre when they were sodden with African mud. I looked around nervously. There were no rhinoceroses on the beach either. The beach was clearly not in Zaïre because Zaïre is landlocked and doesn't have them. I looked at my boots again. They seemed oddly clean. How had that happened? I remembered someone taking my boots away from me and cleaning them. Why would anyone do that? And who? An airport came swimming back to me and I remembered being questioned about my boots and where I had been with them. Zaïre, I said. They took my boots away and returned them to me a few minutes later spotlessly clean and glistening with disinfectant. I remembered thinking at the time that any time I wanted to have my boots really cleaned properly I should remember to fly to New Zealand again. New Zealand. They were quite naturally paranoid about any foreign bacteria being imported into one of the most isolated and unspoiled countries in the world. I tried to remember flying out of New Zealand and couldn't. Therefore, I must still be in New Zealand. Good. I'd narrowed it down a bit. But where?

I stumbled a little woozily up the beach, clambering over the boulders of quietly hallucinatory colours, and then from my new vantage point saw Mark away in the distance on his knees and peering into an old log.

"Moulting little blue penguin," he said when at last I reached him.

119
▼▼▼

"What?" I said. "Where?"

"In the log," he said. "Look."

I peered into the log. A small pair of black eyes peered anxiously back at me from out of a dark ball of ruffled blue fluff.

I sat back heavily on a rock.

"Very nice," I said. "Where are we?"

Mark grinned. "I thought you seemed a bit jet-lagged," he said. "You've been asleep for about twenty minutes."

"Okay," I said irritably "but where are we? I think I've narrowed it down to New Zealand."

"Little Barrier Island," he said. "Remember? We came here this morning by helicopter."

"Ah," I said, "so that answers my next question. It's the afternoon, yes?"

"Yes," said Mark. "It's about four o'clock and we are expected for tea."

I looked up and down the beach again, thunderstruck by this idea.

"Tea?" I said.

"With Mike and Dobby."

"Who?"

"Well, just pretend you know them when we get there, because you spent an hour chatting to them this morning."

"I did?"

"Dobby is the warden of the island."

"And Mike?"

"His wife."

"I see." I thought for a bit. "I know," I said suddenly. "We've come to look for the kakapo. Yes?"

"Correct."

"Will we find one here?"

"Doubt it."

"Then remind me. Why are we here?"

"Because this is one of the only two places where there are definitely kakapos living."

"But we probably won't find one."

"No."

"But we will at least get some tea."

"Yes."

"Well, let's go and get some. Tell me all about it again on the way. But slowly."

"Okay," said Mark. He took a few last pictures of the little blue penguin, a bird which I was destined never to find out anything more about, packed away his Nikons, and together we set off back to the warden's lodge.

"Now that New Zealand is riddled with predators of all kinds," said Mark, "the only possible refuge for kakapos is on islands—and protected islands at that. Stewart Island, in the south, where one or two kakapos are still found, is inhabited and no longer even remotely safe. Any kakapos that are found there are trapped and airlifted to Codfish Island, which is just nearby. They are studied and protected there. In fact, they are so well protected that there's a certain amount of doubt at the moment about whether we'll even be allowed to go there. Apparently there's some furore going on at DOC about—"

"DOC?"

"The New Zealand Department of Conservation. There's a disagreement about whether to let us go there. On the one hand there's a feeling that we might do some good by getting some publicity for the project, and on the other there's a feeling that the birds should not be disturbed on any account. There's only one person available who could help us find the bird and he doesn't want to take us at all."

"Who is he?"

"A freelance kakapo tracker called Arab."

"I see."

"He has a kakapo-tracking dog."

"Hmm. Sounds like the sort of person we need. Is there a lot of work for freelance kakapo trackers? I mean, there aren't a lot of kakapos to track, are there?"

"Forty. In fact, there are three or four kakapo trackers—"

"And three or four kakapo-tracking dogs?"

"Exactly. The dogs are specially trained to sniff out the kakapos. They wear muzzles so that they won't harm the birds. They've been used to trap the kakapos on Stewart Island so that they can then be airlifted to Codfish Island and here to Little Barrier Island by helicopter. First time any of the species have flown at all for thousands, perhaps millions, of years."

"What does a kakapo tracker do when there aren't any kakapos that need tracking?"

"Kills cats."

"Out of frustration?"

"No. Codfish Island was infested with feral cats. In other words, cats that have returned to the wild."

"I always think that's an artificial distinction. I think all cats are wild cats. They just act tame if they think they'll get a saucer of milk out of it. So they kill cats on Codfish Island?"

"Killed them. Every last one. And all the possums and stoats. Anything that moved and wasn't a bird, essentially. It's not very pleasant, but that's how the island was originally, and that's the only way kakapos can survive—in exactly the environment that New Zealand had before man arrived. With no predators. They did the same here on Little Barrier Island too."

At that moment something happened which I found a little startling, until I realised that it had already happened once that day, only in my befuddled jet-lagged state I had completely forgotten about it.

Coming from the beach, we had trudged through thick undergrowth and along rough muddy tracks, across a couple of fields full of sheep, and suddenly emerged into a garden. Not just a garden, but a garden that was meticulously mown and manicured, with immaculate flower beds, well-kempt trees and shrubs, rock gardens, and a little stream with a natty little bridge over it. The effect was that of walking into a slightly suburban Garden of Eden, as if on the Eighth Day God had suddenly got going again and started creating Flymos, secateurs, and those things I can never remember the name of but which are essentially electrically driven pieces of string.

And there, stepping out onto the lawn, was Mike, the warden's wife, with a tray full of tea things, which I fell upon with loud exclamations of delight and hello.

Meanwhile, I had lost Mark altogether. He was standing only a few feet away, but he had gone into a glazed trance which I decided I would go and investigate after I had got to grips with some serious tea. He was probably looking at the birds of which there seemed to be quite a lot in the garden. I chatted cheerfully to Mike, reintroduced myself to her as the vaguely Neanderthal creature she had probably encountered lumbering in a lost daze from the helicopter that morning, and asked her how she coped with living, as she and Dobby had done for eleven and a half years, entirely isolated on this island apart from the occasional nature-loving tourist.

123
▼▼▼

She explained that they had quite a few nature-loving tourists a day, and the worry was that there were too many of them. It was so horribly easy to introduce predators onto the island by mistake, and the damage would be very serious. The tourists who came on organised trips could be managed quite carefully, but the danger came from people coming over to the island on boats and setting up barbecues on the beach. All it would take would be a couple of rats or a pregnant cat, and the work of years would be undone.

I was surprised at the thought that anybody thinking of taking a barbecue to an island beach would necessarily think of including a pregnant cat in their party, but she assured me that it could happen very easily. And virtually every type of boat has rats aboard.

She was a cheerful, sprightly, and robust woman, and I very much suspected that the iron will that had been imposed

on the rugged terrain of the island to turn this acre of it into a ferociously manicured garden was hers.

Gaynor emerged from the neat white clapboard house at this moment with Dobby, whom she had been interviewing on tape. Dobby had originally come to the island eleven and a half years earlier as part of the cat-killing program and stayed on as warden of the reserve, a post from which he was going to have to retire in eighteen months. He was not looking forward to this at all. From where they were standing, in their domain of miniature paradise, a little house in a mainland town seemed desperately constrained and humdrum.

We chatted for a while more and then Gaynor approached Mark to record a description of the garden onto tape, but he gestured her curtly away and returned to the trance he had been in for several minutes now.

This seemed rather odd behaviour from Mark, who was usually a man of mild and genial manners, and I asked him what was up. He muttered something briefly about birds and continued to ignore us.

I looked around again. There certainly were a lot of birds in the garden.

I have to make a confession here, and it's going to sound a little odd coming from someone who has traveled twelve thousand miles and back to visit a parrot, but I am actually not tremendously excited by birds. There are all sorts of things about birds that I find interesting, I suppose, but the things themselves don't really get to me. Hippopotamuses, yes. I'm happy to stare at a hippopotamus till the hippo itself gets bored and wanders away in bemusement. Gorillas, lemurs, dolphins, I will watch entranced for hours, hypnotised as much as anything else by their eyes. But show me a garden full of some of the most exotic birds in the world and I will be just as happy to stand around drinking tea and chatting to people. It gradually dawned on me that this was probably exactly what was happening.

"This," said Mark at last in a low, hollow voice, "is . . ."

I waited patiently.

"Amazing!" he said at last.

Eventually Gaynor prevailed on him to bring himself back from his trance, and he started to talk excitedly about the tuis, the New Zealand pigeons, the bellbirds, the North Island robins, the New Zealand kingfisher, the red-crowned parakeets, the paradise shelducks, and the great crowd of large kakas that was swooping around the garden and jostling one another at the birdbath.

I felt vaguely depressed and also a little fraudulent at being unable to share his excitement, and that evening I fell to wondering why it was that I was so intensely keen to find and see a kakapo and so little bothered by all the other birds.

I think it's its flightlessness.

There is something gripping about the idea that this creature has actually given up doing something that virtually every human being has yearned to do since the very first of us looked upward. I think I find other birds rather irritating for the cocky ease with which they flit through the air as if it was nothing.

I can remember once coming face to face with a free-roaming emu years ago in Sydney zoo. You are strongly warned not to approach them too closely because they can be pretty violent creatures, but once I had caught its eye, I found its irate, staring face absolutely riveting. Because once you look one right in the eye, you have a sudden sense of what the effect has been on the creature of having all the disadvantages of being a bird—absurd posture, a hopelessly scruffy covering of useless feathers, and two useless limbs—without actually being able to do the thing that birds should be able to do, which is to fly. It becomes instantly clear that the bird has gone barking mad.

Here, to digress for a moment, is a little-known fact: one of the more dangerous animals in Africa is, surprisingly enough, the ostrich. Deaths due to ostriches do not excite the public imagination very much because they are essentially so

125
▼▼▼

undignified. Ostriches do not bite because they have no teeth. They don't tear you to pieces because they don't have any forelimbs with claws on them. No, ostriches kick you to death. And who, frankly, can blame them?

The kakapo, though, is not an angry or violent bird. It pursues its own eccentricities rather industriously and modestly. If you ask anybody who has worked with kakapos to describe them, they tend to use words like *innocent* and *solemn,* even when it's leaping helplessly out of a tree. This I find immensely appealing. I asked Dobby if they had given names to the kakapos on the island, and he instantly came up with four of them: Matthew, Luke, John, and Snark. These seemed to be good names for a group of solemnly batty birds.

And then there's the other matter: it's not merely the fact that it's given up that which we all so intensely desire, it's also the fact that it has made a terrible mistake which makes it so compelling. This is a bird you can warm to. I wanted very much to find one.

I became increasingly morose over the next two or three days, because it became clear to us as we traipsed up and down endless hills in the rain that we were not going to find a kakapo on Little Barrier Island. We stopped and admired kakas, long-tailed cuckoos, and yellow-eyed penguins. We endlessly photographed pied shags. One night we saw a morepork, which is a type of owl that got its name from its habit of continually calling for additional pig flesh. But we knew that if we were going to find a kakapo we would need to go to Codfish Island. We would need Arab the freelance kakapo tracker, and we would need the freelance kakapo tracker's kakapo-tracking dog.

And all the signs were that we would not get them. We flew off to Wellington and moped about.

We understood the dilemma facing the Department of Conservation. On the one hand they regarded protection of the kakapos as being of paramount importance, and that meant keeping absolutely everybody who was not vital to the project away from Codfish Island. On the other hand the more people who knew about the animal, the better the chances of mustering more resources to save it. While we were mulling all this over, we were suddenly asked to give a press conference about what we were up to and we happily agreed to this. We talked earnestly and cheerfully to the press about the project. Here was a bird, we explained, that was in its way as extraordinary and unique as the most famous extinct animal of all—the dodo—and it was itself poised on the brink of extinction. It would be far better if it could be famously loved as a survivor than famously regretted, like the dodo.

This seemed to cause some movement within the Department of Conservation, and it transpired that those within it who supported us won their case. A day or two later and we were standing on the tarmac of Invercargill airport at the very south of South Island, waiting for a helicopter. And waiting for Arab. We had won our case, and hoped, a little nervously, that we were right to do so.

Also in our party was a Scotsman from DOC named Ron Tindall. He was politely blunt with us. He said that there was a lot of resentment among the field-workers about our being allowed to go to Codfish, but a directive was a directive, and we were to go. One man, he said, who was particularly set against the whole idea was Arab himself, and it was just as well that we be aware of the fact that he was coming under protest.

A few minutes later Arab himself arrived. I had no idea what I expected a freelance kakapo tracker to look like, but once we saw him, it was clear that if he was hidden in a crowd of a thousand random people, you would still know instantly that he was the freelance kakapo tracker. He was tall, rangy, immensely weather-beaten, and he had a grizzled beard that reached all the way down to his dog, who was called Boss.

He nodded curtly to us and squatted down to fuss with his dog for a moment. Then he seemed to think that perhaps he had been a little curt with us and leaned across Boss to shake our hands. Thinking that he had perhaps overdone this in turn, he then looked up and made a very disgruntled face at the weather. With this brief display of complete social confusion, he revealed himself to be an utterly charming and likeable man.

Nevertheless, the half-hour helicopter trip over to Codfish Island was a little tense. We tried to make cheerful small talk, but this was rendered almost impossible by the deafening thunder of the rotor blades. In a helicopter cockpit you can just about talk to someone who is keen to hear what you have to say, but it is not the best situation in which to try to break the ice.

"What did you say?"

"I just said, 'What did you say?' "

"Ah. What did you say before you said, 'What did you say?' "

"I said, 'What did you say?' "

"I just said, 'Do you come here often?' but let it pass."

At last we lapsed into an awkward, deafened silence that was made all the more oppressive by the heavy bank of storm clouds that was hanging sullenly over the sea.

Soon the sombre bulk of New Zealand's most fiercely protected ark loomed up out of the shining darkness at us: Codfish Island, one of the last refuges of many birds that are hardly to be found anywhere else in the world. Like Little Barrier Island, it has been ruthlessly purged of anything that was not originally to be found there. Even the flightless weka, a fierce and disorderly duck-sized bird, which is native to other parts of New Zealand, has been eradicated. It wasn't a native of Codfish, and it attacked Cook's petrels, which were. The island is surrounded by rough seas and strong currents, so no predator rats are likely to be able to make it from Stewart Island three kilometres away. Food supplies to island workers are stored in rat-proof rooms, packed into rat-proof containers, and rigorously examined before and after transfer. Poison bait is distributed around all possible boat-landing places. There are people ready to swing into immediate fire brigade action to eliminate any rat invasion if a boat wreck occurs.

The helicopter came thudding in to land, and we clambered uneasily out, hunching ourselves down under the rotating blades. We quickly unloaded our bags and walked down and away from the tussocky hillock on which we had landed toward the wardens' hut. Mark and I caught each other's eye for a moment and we realised that we were both still hunched over as we walked. We weren't actually rats, but we felt just about as welcome, and we hoped to God that the expedition was not going to go horribly wrong. Arab stalked silently behind us with Boss, who was now tightly muzzled. Although tracker dogs are rigorously trained not to harm any kakapos they find, they can nevertheless sometimes find them a little too enthusiastically. Even wearing a muzzle, an overeager dog can buffet and injure a bird.

The wardens' hut was a fairly basic wooden building with one large room which served as a kitchen, dining room, sitting room, and workroom, and a couple of small dormitory rooms full of bunks. There were two other field-workers already installed, the eccentrically named, or rather spelled, Phred, who turned out to be the son of Dobby and Mike, and also Trevor. They greeted us quietly and without enthusiasm and let us get on with our unpacking.

Soon we were told that lunch was ready, and we realised that it was time for us seriously to try to improve our general standing around the place. Clearly our hosts did not want to have a bunch of media trendies rampaging around their island frightening the birds with their video cameras and Filofaxes, and they were only slightly mollified by the fact that all we had was one tiny Walkman tape recorder, and that we were being very meek and well behaved and trying not to

129
▼▼▼

order gin and tonics the whole time. The fact that we'd actually brought some beer and whisky with us helped a little.

I suddenly felt extraordinarily cheerful. More cheerful, in fact, than I had felt for the whole of our visit to New Zealand so far. The people of New Zealand are generally terribly *nice*. Everybody we had met so far had been terribly *nice* to us. Terribly nice and eager to please. I realised now that all this relentless niceness and geniality to which we had been subjected had got to me rather badly. New Zealand niceness is not merely disarming, it's decapitating as well, and I had come to feel that if just one more person was pleasant and genial at me, I'd hit him. Now things were suddenly very different and we had work to do. I was determined to get these surly buggers to like us if it killed me.

Over our lunch of tinned ham, boiled potatoes, and beer, we launched a major conversational assault, told them all about our project and why we were doing it, where we'd been so far, what animals we had seen and failed to see, whom we had met, why we were so keen to see the kakapo, how much we appreciated their assistance, and how well we understood their reluctance to have us there, and then we went on to ask intelligent and searching questions about their work, about the island, about the birds, about Boss, and finally, why there was a dead penguin hanging on the tree outside the house.

This seemed to clear the air a little. Our hosts quickly realised that the only way of stopping us talking the whole time was to do some talking themselves. The penguin, Phred explained, was traditional. Every February 28th they hung a dead penguin on a tree. It was a tradition that had only started today and they doubted if they would keep it up, but in the meantime at least it kept the flies off the penguin.

This seemed a thoroughly excellent explanation. We all celebrated it with another glass of beer, and things began at last to move along with a bit more of a swing. In an altogether easier atmosphere, we set out into the forest with Arab and Boss to see if we could at last find one of these birds we had traveled twelve thousand miles to see.

The forest was rotten. That is to say that it was so wet that every fallen tree trunk we had to clamber over cracked open under our feet, branches we clung on to when we lost our footing came away in our hands. We slipped and slithered noisily through the mud and sodden undergrowth, while Arab stalked easily ahead of us, just visible through the trees in his blue-plaid woollen parka. Boss described a chaotic orbit around him, hardly ever visible at all except as an occasional moving flash of blackness through the undergrowth.

He was, however, always audible. Arab had fastened a small bell on to his collar, which rang out clearly through the clean, damp air, as if an invisible and deranged carol singer were cavorting through the forest. The purpose of the bell was to allow Arab to keep track of where Boss was, and also to let him know what the dog was up to. A flurry of agitated rings followed by silence might indicate that Boss had found a kakapo and was standing guard over it. Every time the bell fell silent, we held our breaths, but each time the clanging started up again as Boss found a new avenue in the undergrowth to plunge through. From time to time the bell would suddenly start to ring out more loudly and clearly, and Arab would summon Boss back to him with a quick shout. There would then be a slight pause, which on one occasion enabled Mark and Gaynor and me to catch up with them.

We came tumbling breathless and wet out of the forest to a small clearing, where we found Arab squatting beside Boss, stuffing a small wad of mossy earth up into the cavity of the bell to dampen its sound a little. He squinted up at us with his slow, shy grin and explained that the bell mustn't be too loud or it would only frighten the kakapo away—if there were any in the area.

Did he think there were any around? asked Mark.

"Oh, they're certainly around," said Arab, pulling his fingers through his streaming wet beard to clean the mud off them, "or at least they've been around here today. There's plenty of scent. Boss keeps on finding scent all right, but the scent goes cold. There's been quite a lot of kakapo activity here recently, but not quite recently enough. He's very excited, though. He knows they're definitely around."

He made a fuss of Boss for a few moments, and then explained that there were major problems in training dogs to find kakapos because of the terrible shortage of kakapos to train them on. In the end, he said, it was more realistic to train the dogs not to track anything else. Training was simply a long and tedious process of elimination, which was very frustrating for the dog.

With one last pat, he let go of Boss again, who bounded back off into the bush to carry on snuffling and rummaging for any trace of the one bird he hadn't been trained not to track. Within a few moments he had disappeared from sight, and his muted bell went clanking off into the distance.

We followed a path for a while, which allowed us for the moment to keep up with Arab, while he told us a little about other dogs that he had trained to be hunting dogs, for use in clearing islands of predators. There was one dog he was particularly fond of, which was their top hunting dog, a ferocious killer of an animal. They had taken the dog all the way to Round Island, near Mauritius, with them a few years ago to help with a big rabbit-clearance program. Unfortunately, once it got there, it turned out to be terrified of rabbits and had to be taken home.

It seemed to Arab that most of his recent life had been spent on islands, which was not just a coincidence: island ecologies are so fragile that many island species are endangered, and islands are often used as last places of refuge for mainland animals. Arab himself had tracked many of the twenty-five kakapos that had been found on Stewart Island and airlifted by helicopter in soundproof boxes to Codfish. They always tried to release them in terrain that corresponded as closely as possible to that in which they had been found, in the hope that they would reestablish themselves more easily. But it was very hard to tell how many of the birds were establishing themselves, or even how many had survived here.

The day was wearing on and the light was lengthening. Excitingly, we found some kakapo droppings, which we picked up and crumbled in our fingers and sniffed at in much the same way that a wine connoisseur will savor the bouquet of a fine New Zealand North Island Chardonnay. They have a fine, clean, herbal scent. Almost as excitingly, we found some ferns that a kakapo had chewed at. They clip it and then pull it through their powerful bill so that it leaves a neat ball of curled-up fibre at the end.

A lot less excitingly, we strongly suspected that the day was going to be completely free of any actual kakapos. As the evening gathered in and a light rain began to fall, we turned and trudged the miles we had come back through the forest. We passed the evening in the hut making friends with the whisky bottle and showing off our Nikons.

Toward the end of the evening, Arab mentioned that he hadn't really expected to find a kakapo today at all. They're nocturnal birds and therefore very hard to find during the day. To stand any chance of seeing one at all, you have to go and search when there is just enough light in the sky to let you actually see the thing but when its scent is still fresh on the ground. About five or six in the morning was the time you wanted to go and look for them. Was that okay with us? He stood up and dragged his beard to bed.

Five in the morning is the most horrible time, particularly when your body is still desperately trying to disentangle itself from half a bottle of whisky. We dragged ourselves, cold, crabby, and aching, from our bunks. The noise of sub-machine-gun fire from the main room turned out to be frying bacon, and we tried to revive ourselves with this while the grey morning light began to seep hideously up into the sky outside. I've never understood all this fuss people make

133
▼▼▼

about the dawn. I've seen a few and they're never as good as the photographs, which have the additional advantage of being things you can look at when you're in the right frame of mind, which is usually about lunchtime.

After a lot of sullen fumbling with boots and cameras, we eventually struggled out of the door at about six-thirty and trudged our way back out into the forest. Mark started to point out exciting rare birds to me almost immediately and I told him to take a running jump. A great start to a day of virtually unremitting ornithology. Gaynor asked me to describe the scene as we walked into the forest, and I said that if she poked that microphone in front of me once more, I'd probably be sick over it. I quickly found that I was walking by myself.

After a while I had to admit that the forest wasn't that bad. Cold, wet, and slippery, and continually trying to wrench my legs off at the knees with some bloody tangled root or other, but it also had a kind of fresh glistening quality that wouldn't go away however much I glowered at it. Ron Tindall had joined us this time, and was busy striding his way through the undergrowth in an appallingly robust and Scottish manner, but even this ceased to make my head ache after a while as all the glistening began slowly to work a kind of soothing magic on me. Way ahead of us, half-glimpsed through the misty trees, the blue-plaid parka moved silently like a wraith, following the busy clinking of Boss's bell.

After a longish while of trudging, we caught up with Arab, who had stopped again on a narrow path, and was squatting in the sodden grass.

"There's a fairly recent dropping here," he said, holding up a soft, dark mottled bead for our inspection. "It's got that white on it, which is uric acid, and it hasn't been washed off by the rain or dried out by the sun. That'll disappear in about a day, so this is definitely last night's. This is just where we were, in fact, so I expect we just missed him."

Great, I thought. We could have stayed out a little longer last night, and stayed in bed a lot longer this morning. But the early sun was beginning to glimmer through the trees and there was a lot of fragile beauty business going on where it glistened on the tiny beaded dewdrops on the leaves, so I supposed that it wasn't altogether bad. In fact, there was so much glimmering and glistening and glittering and glinting going on that I began to wonder why it was that so many words that describe what the sun does in the morning begin with the letters "gl," and I mentioned this to Mark, who told me to take a running jump.

Cheered by this little exchange, we set off again. We had hardly gone five yards when Arab, who had already gone fifteen, stopped again. He squatted once more and pointed to some slight signs of digging in the earth.

"That's a very fresh excavation," he said. "Probably last night. Digging for this orchid tuber. You can actually see the beak marks through the bottom here."

I wondered if this was a good time to begin feeling a bit excited and optimistic about the outcome of the day's expedition, but when I did, it started to give me a headache, so I stopped. The damn bird was just stringing us along, and it would be another gloomy evening of sitting in the hut cleaning our lenses and trying to look on the bright side. At least there wouldn't be any whisky this time because we'd drunk it all, so we would be leaving Codfish the following day clearheaded enough to know that we had flown twelve thousand miles to see a bird that hadn't turned up to see us, and all that remained was to fly twelve thousand miles back again and try to find something to write about it. I must have done sillier things in my life, but I couldn't remember when.

The next time Arab stopped, it was for a feather.

"That's a kakapo feather that has dropped," he said, picking it lightly off the side of a bush. "Probably from around the breast by its being quite yellow."

"It's quite downy, isn't it?" said Mark, taking it and twirl-

135
▼▼▼

ing it between his fingers in the misty sunlight. "Do you think it was dropped recently?" he added hopefully.

"Oh yes, it's reasonably fresh," said Arab.

"So this is the closest we've got yet . . . ?"

Arab shrugged. "Yes, I suppose it is," he said. "Doesn't mean we're going to find it, though. You can stand practically on top of one and not see it. The signs are that the kakapo was quite active in the early part of the night, just after we were here. And that's bad news because there was rain during the night, so some of the scent has been washed away. There's plenty of scent around, but it's inconclusive. Still, you never know your luck."

We trudged on. Or perhaps we didn't trudge. Perhaps there was a bit more of a spring in our step, but as half an hour passed, and then an hour, and as the sun gradually crept higher in the sky, Arab was once more a floating wraith far distant from us in the trees ahead, and then we lost him altogether. The spring had certainly dropped from our step. For a while we stumbled on, guided by the very faint sounds of Boss's bell, which was still borne to us on the light breeze sifting through the trees, but then that too stopped and we were lost. Ron was a little way ahead of us, still bounding with rumbustious Scottish gusto, but he too was now floundering for the right direction.

We were clambering over a bank that was thickly covered with ferns and rotten tree trunks, which led down into a wide, shallow gully in the middle of which Ron was standing, looking perplexedly around him. Gaynor lost her footing as she negotiated the muddy slope into the gully, and slithered down it elegantly on her bottom. I got my camera strap caught in the only branch that didn't break off the moment you touched it. Mark stopped to help me disentangle myself. Ron had gone into bounding mode again and was hopping up the far side of the gully calling out for Arab.

"Can you see them?" Mark called out.

A thought struck me. We were lost because Boss's bell had

stopped ringing. The same thought obviously hit Mark simultaneously and we both suddenly called out, "Have they got a kakapo?"

A call came back.

Gaynor turned to us and shouted, "They've got a kakapo!"

Suddenly we were all in rumbustious bounding mode. With much shouting and hallooing, we clambered and slithered our way hectically across the floor of the gully, hauled ourselves up the other side and down into the next gully, on the far side of which, sitting on a mossy bank in front of a steep slope, was a most peculiar tableau.

It took me a moment or two to work out what it was that the scene so closely resembled, and when I realised, I stopped for a moment and then approached more circumspectly.

It was like a Madonna and Child.

Arab was sitting cross-legged on the mossy bank, his long, wet, grizzled beard flowing into his lap. And cradled in his arms, nuzzling gently into his beard, was a large, fat, bedraggled green parrot. Standing by them in quiet attendance, looking at them intently with his head cocked to one side, was Boss, still tightly muzzled.

137
▼▼▼

Duly hushed, we went up to them. Mark was making quiet groaning noises in the back of his throat.

The bird was very quiet and quite still. It didn't appear to be alarmed, but then neither did it appear to be particularly aware of what was happening. The gaze of its large, black, expressionless eye was fixed somewhere in the middle distance. It was holding, lightly but firmly in its bill, the forefinger of Arab's right hand, down which a trickle of blood was flowing, and this seemed to have a calming effect on the bird. Gently, Arab tried to remove it, but the kakapo liked it, and eventually Arab let it stay there. A little more blood flowed down Arab's hand, mingling with the rainwater with which everything was sodden.

To my right, Mark was murmuring about what an honour

it would be to be bitten by a kakapo, which was a point of view I could scarcely understand, but I let it pass.

We asked Arab where he'd found it.

"The dog found it," he said. "Probably about ten yards up this hill, I'd say, under that leaning tree. And when the dog got close, it broke and ran down to just here where I caught it. It's in good condition, though. You can tell that it's close to booming this year because of its spongy chest. That's good news. It means it's establishing itself well after being resettled."

The kakapo shifted itself very slightly in Arab's lap and pushed its face closer into his beard. Arab stroked its damped ruffled feathers very gently.

"It's a bit nervous," he said. "Especially of noise probably more than anything. He looks very bedraggled because of being wet. When Boss first caught up with him, he would have been in a dry roost up there, and probably at the noise of the bell or the dog going too close, the bird broke out and ran down the hill, and was still going when I caught it. It's just gripping me a bit and that's all. If he wanted to put the pressure on . . ." He shrugged. The kakapo clearly had a very powerful bill. It looked like a great horn-plated tin opener welded to its face.

"It's definitely not as relaxed as a lot of birds," muttered Arab. "A lot of birds are really relaxed when you've got them in the hand. I don't want to hold it for too long since it's wet and will get chilled through if the water penetrates to the skin. I think I'd better let it go now."

We stood back. Carefully, Arab leaned forward with the bird, whose big powerful claws stretched out and scrabbled for the ground even before it got there. At last it let go of Arab's finger, steadied its weight on the ground, put its head down, and scuttled off.

That night in the wardens' hut we jubilantly polished off the remaining beers, and pored over the records of all the kaka-

138
▼▼▼

pos that had been transferred to Codfish. Arab had made a note of the identity number of the bird, which had been fastened to its leg: 8-44263. Its name was Ralph. It had been transferred to Codfish Island from Pegasus Harbour, Stewart Island, almost exactly a year ago.

"This is excellent news," exclaimed Ron. "This is really very, very good news indeed. If this kakapo is coming up to booming condition just a year after being relocated, it's the best indication we've had yet that the transfer program is working. You know that we didn't want you to come here, and that we didn't want to track kakapos and risk disturbing them, but as it happens . . . Well, this is very useful information, and very encouraging indeed."

A few days later, when we are standing on top of Kakapo Castle in Fiordland in the shadow of Bill Black's helicopter, we tell Don Merton that we think we've been forgiven.

"Oh yes, I think so," he says. "You may have bumbled around a bit and trodden on a few toes, but you've actually stirred things up a bit as well. The press conference was very effective, and from what I hear, there's an imminent decision coming from quite high up to move the kakapo conservation program to the top of the Department's priority list, which should mean that we get allocated more resources. I just hope it's not all too late.

"There are now twenty-five kakapos on Codfish, but only five of those are females, and that's the crucial point. There's only one kakapo that we know of left on Stewart Island, and that's a male. We keep searching for more females, but we doubt if there are any more. Add those to the fourteen birds on Little Barrier and we have a total of only forty kakapos left altogether.

"And it's so difficult getting the blighters to breed. In the past they bred very slowly because there was nothing else to keep their population stable. If an animal population rises so fast that it outgrows the capacity of its habitat to feed and sustain it, then it plunges right back down again, then back up, back down, and so on. If a population fluctuates too wildly, it doesn't take much of a disaster to tip the species over the edge into extinction. So all the kakapo's peculiar mating habits are just a survival technique as much as anything else. But only because there was no outside competition. Now that they are surrounded by predators, there's very little to keep them alive, other than our direct intervention. As long as we can sustain it."

This reminds me of my motorbike industry analogy, which I have tactfully kept to myself. There are remedies available to motorbike engineers that zoologists do not have. As we tread our way carefully back along the ridge to the helicopter, I ask Don what he feels the long-term prospects for the kakapos really are, and his answer is surprisingly apposite.

"Well," he says in his quiet, polite voice, "anything's possible, and with genetic engineering, who knows. If we can keep them going during our lifespan, it's over to the next generation with their new range of tools and techniques and science to take it from there. All we can do is perpetuate them during our lifetime and try to hand them on in as good a condition as possible to the next generation and hope like heck that they feel the same way about them as we do."

A few minutes later our helicopter rises up above Kakapo Castle, puts its nose down, and heads back up the valleys to Milford Sound, leaving behind a small, scratched depression in the earth and a single, elderly, untouched sweet potato.

BLIND PANIC

SSUMPTIONS ARE the things you don't know you're making, which is why it is so disorienting the first time you take the plug out of a washbasin in Australia and see the water spiraling down the hole the other way around. The very laws of physics are telling you how far you are from home.

In New Zealand even the telephone dials are numbered anti-clockwise. This has nothing to do with the laws of physics—they just do it differently there. The shock is that it had never occurred to you that there was any other way of doing it. In fact, you had never even thought about it at all, and suddenly here it is—different. The ground slips.

Dialing in New Zealand takes quite a bit of concentration because every digit is where you least expect to find it. Try and do it quickly and you will inevitably misdial because

your automatic habit jumps in and takes over before you
have a chance to stop it. The habit of telephone dials is so
deep that it has become an assumption, and you don't even
know you're making it.

China is in the Northern Hemisphere, so its washbasins
drain clockwise, like ours. Their telephone dials are numbered like ours. Both those things are familiar. But every
single other thing is different, and the assumptions that you
don't know you're making will only get you into trouble and
confusion.

I had a kind of inkling that this would be the case from
what little I knew of other people's experiences in China. I
sat in the plane on the long flight to Beijing trying to unravel
my habits, to unthink as it were, and feeling slightly twitchy
about it.

I started buying copious quantities of aftershave. Each
time the duty-free trolley came around, I bought a bottle. I
had never done anything like it before in my life. My normal,
instinctive reaction had always been just to shake my head
and carry on reading my magazine. This time I thought it
would be more Zen-like to say, "Yes, all right. What have
you got?" I was not the only person I caught by surprise.

"Have you gone completely mad?" Mark asked me as I
slipped a sixth different bottle into my hand baggage.

"I'm trying to challenge and subvert my own fundamental
assumptions as to what constitutes rationally constructed behaviour."

"Does that mean yes?"

"I mean that I'm just trying to loosen up a bit," I said. "An
airplane doesn't give you much scope for arbitrary and alter-
native types of behaviour, so I'm just making the most of the
opportunities that are offered."

"I see."

Mark shifted uncomfortably in his seat and frowned
deeply into his book.

"What are you going to do with all that stuff?" he asked a while later over an airline meal.

"Dunno," I said. "It's a problem, isn't it?"

"Tell me, are you feeling nervous about something?"

"Yes."

"What?"

"China."

In the middle of one of the biggest, longest, noisiest, dirtiest thoroughfares in the world lives the reincarnation of a drowned princess, or rather, two hundred reincarnations of a drowned princess.

Whether these are two hundred different reincarnations of the same drowned princess, or the individual reincarnations of two hundred different drowned princesses, is something that the legends are a little vague about, and there are no reliable statistics on the incidence of princess-drownings in the area available to help clear the matter up.

If they are all the same drowned princess, then she must have led a life of exquisite sinfulness to have had the conditions of her current lives repeatedly inflicted on her. Her reincarnations are constantly being mangled in ships' propellers, snared in fishermen's nets full of hooks, blinded, poisoned, and deafened.

The thoroughfare in question is the Yangtze River, and the reincarnated princess is the baiji, the Yangtze river dolphin.

"How do you rate our chances of seeing a dolphin?" I asked Mark.

"I haven't the faintest idea," he said. "It's very hard to get information about anything out of China, and most of it's confusing. But the dolphins are to be found—or not—in just a few parts of the Yangtze. The main one is a stretch of the river about two hundred kilometres long centered on a town called Tongling in Anhui province. That's where there are people working on saving the baiji, and that's the main place

143
▼▼▼

we're headed for. We get to Tongling by boat from Nanjing, where there's a man called Professor Zhou, who's a major authority on the animal. We get to Nanjing by train from Shanghai. We get to Shanghai by plane from Beijing. We've got a couple of days in Beijing first to get acclimatised and see if any of the travel arrangements are actually going to work out. We've got thousands of miles to cover and travel is supposed to be insanely difficult.

"Do we have much leeway if things go wrong?" I asked. "Which days are Professor Zhou and the others expecting us?"

"Expecting us?" said Mark. "What do you mean? They've never heard of us. You can't actually contact anyone in China. We'll be lucky to find them and even luckier if they agree to talk to us. In fact, I'm only half-certain they exist. We're going into completely unknown territory."

We both peered out of the window. Darkness was falling over the largest nation on earth.

144
▼▼▼

"There's just one last bottle left, sir," said the cabin steward to me at that moment. "Would you like it before we close up the duty-free? Then you'll have the complete range."

It was quite late at night as a rickety minibus delivered us to our hotel on the outskirts of Beijing. At least, I think it was the outskirts. We had no point of reference by which to judge what kind of area it was. The streets were wide and tree-lined but eerily silent. Any motor vehicle made a single and particular growl instead of merging with a general traffic hum. The streetlights had no diffusing glass covers, so the light they shed was sharp, highlighting each leaf and branch and precisely delineating their shapes against the walls. Passing cyclists cast multiple interweaving shadows on the road around them. The sense of moving in a geometric web was added to by the clack of billiard balls as they cannoned across small tables set up under the occasional street lamp.

The hotel was set in a small network of narrow side streets,

and its facade was wildly decorated with the carved red dragons and gilded pagoda shapes that are the familiar stereotypes of China. We hefted our bags full of camera equipment, recording gear, clothes, and aftershave into the lobby, past the long glass counter displays of carved chopsticks, ginseng, and herbal aphrodisiacs, and waited to check in.

I noticed an odd thing. It was one of those tiny little disorienting details, like the telephone dials in New Zealand, that tell you you are in a very distant and foreign country. I knew that the Chinese traditionally hold their table-tennis paddles the way we hold cigarettes. What I did not know was that they also hold their cigarettes the way we hold table-tennis paddles.

Our rooms were small. I sat on the edge of my bed, which was made for someone of half my height, and laid out my bewildering collection of aftershave bottles in a neat line next to two large and ornately decorated red and gold thermos flasks that were already standing on the bedside table. I wondered how I was going to get rid of them. I decided to sleep on the problem. I hoped I would be able to. I read a note in the hotel's directory of guest services with foreboding. It said: "No dancing, clamoring, quarreling, fisticuffing, or indulging in excessive drinking and creating disturbances in public places for the sake of keeping a peaceful and comfortable environment. Guests are not permitted to bring pets and poultry into the hotel."

The morning presented me with a fresh problem. I wanted to clean my teeth, but was a little suspicious of the delicate brown colour of the water leaking from the washbasin taps. I investigated the large flamboyant thermos flasks, but they were full of very hot water, for making tea. I poured some water from a thermos into a glass and left it to cool while I went to meet Mark and Chris Muir, our sound engineer, for a late breakfast.

Mark had already been trying to get through to Nanjing

145
▼▼▼

on the phone in an attempt to contact Professor Zhou, the baiji dolphin expert, and had come to the conclusion that it simply couldn't be done. We had two days to kill before our flight to Shanghai, so we might just as well be tourists for a bit.

I returned to my room to clean my teeth at last, to discover that the room maid had washed the glass I'd left out to cool, and refilled the thermoses with freshly boiling water.

I felt rather cast down by this. I tried pouring some water from one glass to another to cool it down, but even after doing this for a while the water was still hot, and the toothbrush wilted in my mouth.

I realised that I was going to have to come up with some serious strategic thinking if I was going to get to clean my teeth. I refilled the glass, carefully stuck it out of sight in the back of a cupboard, and then tried to get rid of one of the bottles of aftershave by hiding it under the bed.

We put on our sunglasses and cameras and went and spent the day looking at the Great Wall at Badaling, an hour or so outside Beijing. It looked to be remarkably freshly built for such an ancient monument, and probably the parts we saw had been.

I remembered once, in Japan, having been to see the Gold Pavilion Temple in Kyoto and being mildly surprised at quite how well it had weathered the passage of time since it was first built in the fourteenth century. I was told it hadn't weathered well at all, and had in fact been burned to the ground twice in this century.

"So it isn't the original building?" I had asked my Japanese guide.

"But yes, of course it is," he insisted, rather surprised at my question.

"But it's been burned down?"

"Yes."

"Twice."

"Many times."

"And rebuilt."

"Of course. It is an important and historic building."

"With completely new materials."

"But of course. It was burned down."

"So how can it be the same building?"

"It is always the same building."

I had to admit to myself that this was in fact a perfectly rational point of view, it merely started from an unexpected premise. The idea of the building, the intention of it, its design, are all immutable and are the essence of the building. The intention of the original builders is what survives. The wood of which the design is constructed decays and is replaced when necessary. To be overly concerned with the original materials, which are merely sentimental souvenirs of the past, is to fail to see the living building itself.

I couldn't feel entirely comfortable with this view, because it fought against my basic Western assumptions, but I did see the point.

I don't know whether this principle lies beneath the rebuilding of the Great Wall, because I couldn't find anybody who understood the question. The rebuilt section was swarming with tourists and Coca-Cola booths and shops where you can buy Great Wall T-shirts and electric pandas, and this may also have had something to do with it.

We returned to our hotel.

The maid had found my hidden glass of water and washed it. She must have searched hard for it because she had also found the bottle of aftershave under the bed and had placed it neatly back on the table by the others.

"Why don't you just use the stuff?" asked Mark.

"Because I've smelled them all and they're horrid."

"You could give them to people for Christmas."

"I don't want to carry them around the world till then."

"Remind me again why you bought them."

"I can't remember. Let's go to dinner."

We went to a restaurant called Crispy Fried Duck for din-

ner, and walking back through the city centre afterward we came to a square called Tiananmen.

I should explain that this was October 1988. I had never heard the name Tiananmen Square, and neither had most of the world.

The square is huge. Standing in it at night, you have very little idea of where its boundaries are, they fade into the distance. At one end is the gateway to the Forbidden City, the Tiananmen Gate, from which the great iconic portrait of Chairman Mao gazes out across the vastness of the square, out toward its furthest point, where there stands the mausoleum in which his body lies in state.

In between these two, beneath his gaze, the mood was festive. Huge topiary bushes carved into the figures of cartoon animals had been imported into the square to celebrate the Olympics.

The square was not full or crowded—it would take many tens or even hundreds of thousands of people to achieve that —but it was busy. Families were out with their children (or more usually, with their single child). They walked around, chatting with friends, milling about easily and freely as if the square were their own garden, letting their children wander off and play with others without an apparent second thought. It would be hard to imagine anything of the kind in any of the great squares of Europe, and inconceivable in America.

In fact, I cannot remember any time that I have felt so easy and relaxed in a busy public place, particularly at night. The background static of wary paranoia that you take with you as a matter of unconscious habit when you step out into the streets of Western cities made itself suddenly apparent by falling silent. It was a quite magical silence.

I have to say, though, that this was probably the only time we felt so easy in China, or indeed easy at all. For most of the time we found China baffling and exasperating and per-

petually opaque; but that evening, in Tiananmen Square, was easy. So the greatest bewilderment of all came a few months later when Tiananmen Square underwent that brutal transformation that occurs in the public mind to the sites of all catastrophes: they become reference points in time instead of actual places. "Before Tiananmen Square" was when we were there. "After Tiananmen Square" was after the tanks rolled in.

We returned to the square early the following morning, while the air was still damp and misty, and joined the queues that line up round the square each day to file into the mausoleum and past the body of Chairman Mao, lying in state in a perspex box.

The length of the queue beggared belief. It zigzagged backward and forward across the square, each new fold of it looming up at you from out of the mist and disappearing into it again, rank after rank, line after line. People stood in line about three or four abreast, shuffled briskly forward across the square, made a turn and shuffled briskly back, again and again, all under the orders of officials who paraded up and down in flared trousers and yellow parkas, barking through megaphones. The easy atmosphere of the previous evening had vanished in the dreary morning mist, and the square was degraded into a giant marshaling yard.

We joined the line after some hesitation, half-expecting that we might be there all day, but we were kept constantly on the move by the barking marshals, and even found that we were accelerating as we got closer to the front. Less than three hours after we had tagged on to the end of the line, we were hurried into the red-pile-carpeted inner sanctum and ran past the tiny, plump, waxy body as respectfully as we could.

The queue, which had been so tightly and rigorously controlled as it was lined up to be fed into the mausoleum, disintegrated among the souvenir stalls as it emerged from

the other side. I imagined that from the air the building must resemble a giant mincing machine.

The whole square and all the surrounding streets were served by a network of public address speakers, out of which music was pumped all day long. It was hard to make out what it was most of the time because the system was pretty ropey, and the sound just thumped and blared and echoed indecipherably around us, but as we climbed to the top of the Tiananmen Gate a few minutes later, we began to hear much more clearly what it was we were listening to.

The Tiananmen Gate, I should first explain, is a tall, flat-fronted structure with arches at the bottom through which you pass into the Forbidden City, and a large balcony across the top, behind which is a series of meeting rooms.

The Gate was built during the Ming Dynasty and used by the Emperors for making public appearances and proclamations. The Gate, like Tiananmen Square, has always been a major point of focus in the political history of China. If you

150
▼▼▼

climb up to the balcony, you can stand on the spot from which, on October 1, 1949, Chairman Mao proclaimed the founding of the People's Republic of China. The spot is clearly marked, and there is an exhibition of photographs of the event clustered around it.

The view across the immensity of Tiananmen Square from here is extraordinary. It is like looking across a plain from the side of a mountain. In political terms the view is more astounding yet, encompassing as it does a nation that comprises almost one-quarter of the population of this planet. All of the history of China is symbolically focused here, at this very point, and it is hard, as you stand there, not to be transfixed by the power of it. It is hard, also, not to be profoundly moved by the vision of the peasant from Shao-Shan who seized that power in the name of the people and whom the people still revere, in spite of the atrocities of the Cultural Revolution, as the father of their nation.

And while we were standing on this spot, the spot where Mao stood when he proclaimed the founding of the People's Republic of China, the music we were having played at us by the public address system was first "Viva España" and then the "Theme from Hawaii Five-O."

It was hard to avoid the feeling that somebody, somewhere, was missing the point. I couldn't even be sure that it wasn't me.

We flew to Shanghai the next day and began to think about the dolphins toward which we were slowly edging our way across China. We went to think about them in the bar of the Peace Hotel. This turned out not to be a good place to think because you couldn't hear yourself doing it, but we wanted to see the place anyway.

The Peace Hotel is a spectacular remnant of the days when Shanghai was one of the most glamorous and cosmopolitan ports in the world. In the Thirties the hotel was known as the Cathay, and was the most sumptuous place in town. This was where people came to glitter at one another. In one of its suites Noël Coward wrote a draft of *Private Lives*.

Now the paint is peeling, the lobby is dark and draughty, the posters advertising the World Famous Peace Hotel Jazz Band are written in felt tip and Scotch-taped onto the paneling, but the ghost of the Cathay's former grandeur still lurks high up among the dusty chandeliers, wondering what's been going on for the last forty years.

The bar was a dark, low-ceilinged room just off the lobby. The World Famous Peace Hotel Jazz Band was out for the evening, but a deputy band was playing in their place. The promise is that this is one of the only places in the world where you will still hear the music of the Thirties played as it was played, where it was played. Maybe the World Famous combo keeps the promise, but their deputies did not. They banged their way through endless repetitions of "Edel-

weiss," "Greensleeves," and "Auld Lang Syne," interspersed with the occasional bash at "New York, New York," "Chicago," and "I Left My Heart in San Francisco."

There were two odd things about this. First of all, this wasn't just for the tourists. This was the music we heard everywhere in China, particularly the first three titles: on the radio, in shops, in taxis, in trains, in the great ferries that steam continually up and down the Yangtze. Usually it was played by Richard Clayderman. For anyone who has ever wondered who in the world buys Richard Clayderman records, it's the Chinese, and there are a billion of them.

The other odd thing was that music was clearly completely foreign to them. Well, obviously it was foreign music, so that's not altogether surprising, but it was as if they were playing from a phrase book. Every extempore flourish the trumpeter added, every extra fill on the drums, were all crashingly and horribly wrong. I suppose that Indians must have felt this hearing George Harrison playing the sitar in the Sixties, but then, after a brief indulgence, so did everybody else; clumsy replications of Indian music never supplanted the popular music of the West. When the Chinese listened avidly to mangled renditions of "Auld Lang Syne" and "Little Brown Jug," they were obviously hearing something very different than what I was hearing and I couldn't work out what it was.

Traveling in China, I began to find that it was the sounds I was hearing that confused and disoriented me most.

It occurred to me, as we tried to find a table in one of the more muffled corners of the bar, that the dolphins we had come to look for must be suffering from the same kind of problem. Their senses must be completely overwhelmed and confused.

To begin with, the baiji dolphin is half-blind.

The reason for this is that there is nothing to see in the Yangtze. The water is so muddy now that visibility is not

much more than a few centimetres, and as a result the baiji's eyes have atrophied through disuse.

Curiously enough, it is often possible to tell something about the changes that have occurred during an animal's evolution from the way in which its fetus develops. It's a sort of action replay.

The baiji's eyes, feeble as they are, are placed quite high up on its head to make the most of the only light that ever reaches them, i.e., from directly above. Most other dolphins have their eyes much lower down the sides of their heads, from where they can see all around them, and below; and this is exactly where you will find the eyes on a young baiji fetus.

As the fetus grows, however, its eyes gradually migrate up the sides of its head, and the muscles that would normally pull the eyeball downward don't even bother to develop. You can't see anything downward.

It may be, therefore, that the entire history of soil erosion into the Yangtze can be charted in the movement of a single baiji fetus's eyes. (It may also be that the baiji arrived into an already turbid Yangtze from somewhere else and just adapted to its new environment; we don't know. Either way, the Yangtze has become much muddier during the history of the baiji species, mostly because of human activity.)

As a consequence, the baiji had to use a different sense to find its way around. It relies on sound. It has incredibly acute hearing, and "sees" by echolocation, emitting sequences of tiny clicks and listening for the echoes. It also communicates with other baijis by making whistling noises.

Since man invented the engine, the baiji's river world must have become a complete nightmare.

China has a pretty poor road system. It has railways, but they don't go everywhere, so the Yangtze (which in China is called the Chang Jiang, or "Long River") is the country's main highway. It's crammed with boats all the time, and

153
▼▼▼

always has been—but they used to be sailing boats. Now the river is constantly churned up by the engines of rusty old tramp steamers, container ships, giant ferries, passenger liners, and barges.

I said to Mark, "It must be continuous bedlam under the water."

"What?"

"I said it's hard enough for us to talk in here with this band going on, but it must be continuous bedlam under the water."

"Is that what you've been sitting here thinking all this time?"

"Yes."

"I thought you'd been quiet."

"I was trying to imagine what it would be like to be a blind man trying to live in a discotheque. Or several competing discotheques."

"Well, it's worse than that, isn't it?" Mark said. "Dolphins rely on sound to see with."

"All right, so it would be like a deaf man living in a discotheque."

"Why?"

"All the stroboscopic lights and flares and mirrors and lasers and things. Constantly confusing information. After a day or two you'd become completely bewildered and disoriented and start to fall over the furniture."

"Well, that's exactly what's happening, in fact. The dolphins are continually being hit by boats or mangled in their propellers or tangled in fishermen's nets. A dolphin's echolocation is usually good enough for it to find a small ring on the sea bed, so things must be pretty serious if it can't tell that it's about to be brained by a boat.

"Then, of course, there's all the sewage, the chemical and industrial waste and artificial fertiliser that's being washed into the Yangtze, poisoning the water and poisoning the fish."

"So," I said, "what do you do if you are either half-blind, or half-deaf, living in a discotheque with a stroboscopic light show, where the sewers are overflowing, the ceiling and the fans keep crashing on your head, and the food is bad?"

"I think I'd complain to the management."

"They can't."

"No. They have to wait for the management to notice."

A little later I suggested that, as representatives of the management so to speak, perhaps we ought to try to hear what the Yangtze actually sounded like under the surface—to record it in fact. Unfortunately, since we'd only just thought of it, we didn't have an underwater microphone with us.

"Well, there's one thing we can do," said Chris. "There's a standard technique in the BBC for waterproofing a microphone in an emergency. What you do is you get the microphone and you stuff it inside a condom. Either of you got any condoms with you?"

"Er, no."

"Nothing lurking in your sponge bags?"

"No."

"Well, we'd better go shopping, then."

By now I was beginning to think in sound pictures. There are two very distinctive sounds in China, three if you count Richard Clayderman.

The first is spitting. Everybody spits. Wherever you are you continually hear the sound: the long-drawn-out, sucking, hawking noise of mucus being gathered up into the mouth, followed by the hissing launch of the stuff through the air, and, if you're lucky, the ping of it hitting a spittoon, of which there are many. Every room has at least one. In one hotel lobby I counted a dozen strategically placed in corners and alcoves. In the streets of Shanghai there is a plastic spittoon sunk into the pavement on every street corner, filled with cigarette butts, litter, and thick, curling, bubbly mucus. You will also see many signs saying NO SPITTING, but since these are in English rather than Chinese, I suspect that they are of cosmetic value only. I was told that spitting in the street was actually an offence now, with a fine attached to it. If it were ever enforced, I think that the entire economy of China would tilt on its axis.

The other sound is the Chinese bicycle bell. There is only one type of bell, and it's made by the Seagull Company, which also makes Chinese cameras. The cameras, I think, are not the world's best, but the bicycle bells may well be, as they are built for heavy use. They are big, solid, spinning chrome drums and have a great resounding chime to them which you hear ringing out through the streets continuously.

Everyone in China rides bicycles. Private cars are virtually unheard of, so the traffic in Shanghai consists of trolley buses, taxis, vans, trucks, and tidal waves of bicycles.

The first time you stand at a major intersection and watch, you are convinced that you are about to witness major carnage. Crowds of bicycles are converging on the intersection from all directions. Trucks and trolley buses are already barreling through it. Everyone is ringing a bell or sounding a horn and no one is showing any signs of stopping. At the moment of inevitable impact, you close your eyes and wait for the horrendous crunch of mangled metal but, oddly, it never comes.

It seems impossible. You open your eyes. Several dozen bicycles and trucks have all passed straight through one another as if they were merely beams of light.

Next time you keep your eyes open and try to see how the trick's done; but however closely you watch you can't untangle the dancing, weaving patterns the bikes make as they seem to pass insubstantially through one another, all ringing their bells.

In the Western world, to ring a bell or sound a horn is usually an aggressive thing to do. It carries a warning or an instruction: "Get out of the way," "Get a move on," or

"What the hell kind of idiot are you, anyway?" If you hear a lot of horns blowing on a New York street, you know that people are in a dangerous mood.

In China, you gradually realise, the sound means something else entirely. It doesn't mean, "Get out of my way, asshole," it just means a cheerful "Here I am." Or rather it means, "Here I am here I am here I am here I am here I am . . . ," because it is continuous.

It occurred to me as we threaded our way through the crowded, noisy streets looking for condoms that perhaps Chinese cyclists also navigated by a form of echolocation.

"What do you think?" I asked Mark.

"I think you've been having some very strange ideas since we came to China."

"Yes, but if you're weaving along in a pack of cyclists, and everyone's ringing their bells, you probably get a very clear spatial perception of where everybody is. You notice that none of them have lights on their bicycles?"

"Yes . . ."

"I read somewhere that the writer James Fenton tried riding a bike with a light on it in China one night and the police stopped him and told him to take it off. They said, 'How would it be if everyone went around with lights on their bicycles?' So I think they must navigate by sound. The other thing that's extraordinary about cyclists is their inner peace."

"What?"

"Well, I don't know what else it can be. It's the extraordinary, easy unconcern with which a cyclist will set off directly across the path of an oncoming bus. They just miss a collision which, let's face it, would not harm the bus very much, and though they only miss by about an inch, the cyclist doesn't appear even to notice."

"What is there to notice? The bus missed him."

"But only just."

"But it missed him. That's the point. I think that we get alarmed by close scrapes because they're an invasion of space

as much as anything else. The Chinese don't worry about privacy or personal space. They probably think we're neurotic about it."

The Friendship Store seemed like a promising place to buy condoms, but we had a certain amount of difficulty in getting the idea across. We passed from one counter to another in the large open-plan department store, which consists of many different individual booths, stalls, and counters, but no one was able to help us.

We started at the stalls that looked as if they sold medical supplies, but had no luck. By the time we had got to the stalls that sold bookends and chopsticks, we knew we were on to a loser, but at least we found a young shop assistant who spoke English.

We tried to explain to her what it was we wanted, but seemed to reach the limit of her vocabulary pretty quickly. I got out my notebook and drew a condom very carefully, including the little extra balloon on the end.

She frowned at it, but still didn't get the idea. She brought us a wooden spoon, a candle, a sort of paper knife, and, surprisingly enough, a small porcelain model of the Eiffel Tower and then at last lapsed into a posture of defeat.

Some other girls from the stall gathered round to help, but they were also defeated by our picture. At last I plucked up the bravado to perform a delicate little mime and at last the penny dropped.

"Ah!" the first girl said, suddenly wreathed in smiles. "Ah yes!"

They all beamed delightedly at us as they got the idea.

"You do understand?" I asked.

"Yes! Yes, I understand."

"Do you have any?"

"No," she said. "Not have."

"Oh."

"But, but, but . . ."

"Yes?"

"I say you where you go, okay?"

"Thank you very much. Thank you."

"You go 616 Nanjing Road. Okay. Have there. You ask 'rubberover.' Okay?"

"Rubberover?"

"Rubberover. You ask. They have. Okay. Have nice day." She giggled happily about this with her hand over her mouth.

We thanked them again, profusely, and left with much waving and smiling. The news seemed to have spread very quickly around the store, and everybody waved at us. They seemed terribly pleased to have been asked.

When we reached 616 Nanjing Road, which turned out to be another, smaller department store, and not a knocking shop as we had been half-suspecting, our pronunciation of "rubberover" seemed to let us down and produce another wave of baffled incomprehension.

This time I went straight for the mime that had served us so well before, and it seemed to do the trick at once. The shop assistant, a middle-aged lady with severe hair, marched straight to a cabinet of drawers, brought us back a packet, and placed it triumphantly on the counter in front of us.

Success, we thought. But then we opened the packet and found it to contain a bubble sheet of pills.

"Right idea," said Mark with a sigh. "Wrong method."

We were quickly floundering again as we tried to explain to the now slightly affronted lady that it wasn't precisely what we were after. By this time a crowd of about fifteen onlookers had gathered around us, some of whom, I was convinced, had followed us all the way from the Friendship Store.

One of the things that you quickly discover in China is that we are all at the zoo. If you stand still for a minute, people will gather round and stare at you. The unnerving

thing is that they don't stare intently or inquisitively, they just stand there, often right in front of you, and watch you as blankly as if you were a dog-food commercial.

At last a young and pasty-faced man with glasses pushed through the crowd and said he spoke a little English and could he help?

We thanked him and said yes, we wanted to buy some condoms, some "rubberovers," and we would be very grateful if he could explain that for us.

He looked puzzled, picked up the rejected packet lying on the counter in front of the affronted shop assistant, and said, "Not want rubberover. This better."

"No," Mark said. "We definitely want rubberover, not pills."

"Why want rubberover? Pill better."

"You tell him," said Mark.

"It's to record dolphins," I said. "Or not the actual dolphins in fact. What we want to record is the noise in the Yangtze that . . . It's to go over the microphone, you see, and . . ."

"Oh, just tell him you want to fuck someone," muttered Chris Scottishly. "And you can't wait."

But by now the young man was edging nervously away from us, suddenly realising that we were dangerously insane and should simply be humored and escaped from. He said something hurriedly to the shop assistant and backed away into the crowd.

The shop assistant shrugged, scooped up the pills, opened another drawer, and pulled out a packet of condoms.

We bought nine, just to be on the safe side.

"They've got aftershave as well," said Mark, "if you're running out."

I had already managed to dispose of one bottle of aftershave in the hotel in Beijing, and I hid another under the seat on the train to Nanjing.

160
▼▼▼

"You know what you're doing?" said Mark as he spotted me. I'd thought he was asleep.

"Yes. I'm trying to get rid of this bloody stuff. I wish I'd never bought it."

"No, it's more than that. When an animal strays into new territory, where it doesn't feel at home, it marks its passage with scent, just to lay claim. You remember the ring-tailed lemurs in Madagascar? They've got scent glands in their wrists. They rub their tails between their wrists and then wave their tails in the air to spread the scent around, just to occupy the territory. That's why dogs pee against lampposts as well. You're just scent-marking your way around China. Old habits die hard."

"Does anyone happen to know," asked Chris, who had been lolling sleepily against the window for an hour or so, "what the Chinese for Nanjing actually *looks* like? I only ask so as we'll know when we've got there."

In Nanjing we had our first sight of the river. Although Shanghai is known as the gateway to the Yangtze, it isn't actually on it, but is on a connecting river called the Huangpu. Nanjing is on the Yangtze itself.

It is a grim town, or at least we found it to be so. The sense of alien dislocation gathered us more tightly into its grip. We found the people to be utterly opaque; they would either stare at us or ignore us. I was reminded of a conversation I had had with a Frenchman on the plane to Beijing.

"It is difficult to talk to the Chinese people," he had said. "Partly it is the language, if you do not speak Chinese, but also, you know, they have been through many, many things. So they think it is safer perhaps to ignore you. If they talk to you or do not talk to you, they are paid the same whatever, so, *pfffft*. I think if they get to know you, they talk a little more, perhaps, but *pfffft*."

The sense of dislocation was sharpened by the presence, in the centre of town, of a single major Western-style high-rise

161
▼▼▼

hotel, called the Jing Ling. It was an anonymously grand conference-holding, revolving-bar-and-atrium-ridden modern hotel of the sort that generally I heartily dislike, but suddenly it was like an oasis to us.

We made straight for the revolving top-floor bar like rats from a sack and sat huddled for safety around a cluster of gin and tonics. After twenty minutes or so of sitting in these unexpectedly familiar surroundings, we found, as we gazed out of the panoramic windows at the vast, alien, darkened city which turned slowly around us, that we felt like astronauts in a vast, warm life-support system, looking out over the hostile and barren terrain of another planet.

We were all seized with a sudden desire not to have to go out there anymore, not to have to be stared at, ignored, spat at, or have our personal space invaded by bicycles. Unfortunately, the Jing Ling had no available rooms, and we were ejected into the night to find lodging in an altogether grimmer crumbling hotel on the outskirts, where we sat and thought, once more, about the dolphins out in their filthy river and how we were to make our recording.

162
▼▼▼

On a day darkened with drizzle, we stood on the bank of the Yangtze, watching the great drifting sea of sludge which flows sullenly from the depths of China. The only colour in a heavy landscape of dark brown shading to grey, against which long, black, smoke-belching silhouettes of diesel-engined junks thudded and growled up the river, was a little pink knotted condom dangling limply on the end of a cable attached to Chris's tape recorder. The half-heard swish of unseen multitudes of bicycles was like the distant drumming of hooves. From here the bewilderment of Shanghai seemed like a remote warm memory of home.

The river was not deep enough at the bank for our sound experiment, and we slogged our way through the accumulating rain toward the docks in search of deeper water. We shook our heads at the occasional importunate cries from

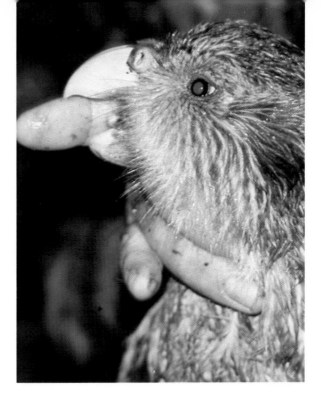

Ralph the kakapo
biting Arab the
kakapo tracker's
finger for comfort.

A kea with its windscreen-wiper-ripping beak.

Below left: A yellow-eyed penguin looking doubtful.

Below right: Arab the kakapo tracker with Boss, his kakapo-tracking dog.

Qi-Qi, the only
baiji dolphin
in captivity. It
was found by
fishermen in
Dongting Lake in
1980, severely
injured by a
fishing hook.
They took it to
the Institute of
Hydrobiology in
Wuhan, where it
was nursed back
to health with the
help of traditional
Chinese medicine.

Douglas trying to photograph a bush from the inside.

The echo parakeet—one of the rarest birds in the world.

Rodrigues fruit bats in the captive breeding center on Mauritius.

A rare moment of excitement in the hippo pool.

Mark demonstrating the most effective way of catching the world's most common disease after tooth decay.

passing bicycle-driven rickshaws, being too sunk in gloom to admit even the possibility of relief.

We found a temporarily deserted passenger ferry lolling against the creaking dock and trudged up the gangplank. The ferries are big, hulking, five-decker wedges, which look like immense, soiled slices of lemon gâteau grinding daily up and down the Yangtze, each carrying upwards of a thousand cramped passengers and playing Richard Clayderman at them. We found our way through a series of bulkhead doors to a deck that overlooked the river, where Chris tried hopelessly to dangle the little pink thing with its button microphone down into the murky waters. It would scarcely reach, was blown about by the wind, and when at last it dropped down to the water, it sat perkily on top of it.

There was another deck below us, but it proved difficult to find—the innards of the boat continually deflected us with bolted doors. At last we solved the maze of it and emerged once again overlooking the river, several feet lower.

The microphone still would not sink into the thick brown water until we weighted it down with my hotel room key from Beijing, which I discovered inadvertently about my person. The microphone, wrapped in its condom, settled into the depths and Chris started to record.

Boat after boat crawled thunderously past us up the river. They were mostly twenty- or thirty-foot soot-black junks, whose small crews regarded us sometimes with perplexed curiosity and sometimes not at all. At the back of each junk an aged diesel engine juddered and bellowed as it poured black clouds into the air and drove the screw beneath the water.

After we had been on the deck a few minutes, a member of the ferry's crew suddenly arrived and expressed surprise at seeing us there. We did not, of course, speak Mandarin, but the question "What the hell do you think you're doing?" has a familiar ring in any language.

The mere idea of even attempting to account for ourselves

defeated us. We settled instead for explaining, by means of elaborate mime and sign language, that we were barking mad. This worked. He accepted it, but then hung around in the background to watch us anyway. At last Chris hauled the apparatus up out of the water, dried it off, and showed it to him. As soon as the crewman recognised that it was a condom we had been dangling in the water, it seemed as if some light dawned.

"Ah!" he said. "Ficky Ficky!" He grinned happily and plunged his forefinger in and out of his other fist. "Ficky ficky!"

"Yes," we agreed. "Ficky ficky."

Pleased that all was clear now, he wandered off and left us to it as, each in turn, we listened to the tape over headphones.

The sound we heard wasn't exactly what I had expected. Water is a very good medium for the propagation of sound and I had expected to hear clearly the heavy, pounding reverberations of each of the boats that had gone thundering by us as we stood on the deck. But water transmits sound even better than that, and what we were hearing was everything that was happening in the Yangtze for many, many miles around, jumbled cacophonously together.

Instead of hearing the roar of each individual ship's propeller, what we heard was a sustained shrieking blast of pure white noise, in which nothing could be distinguished at all.

Happily, Professor Zhou did exist. Not only did he exist, but when Mark went to look for him at Nanjing University (I was ill that day), he was actually in and agreed to come and have dinner with us at the Jing Ling Hotel (by which time I was better because it was quite a good restaurant).

He was a polite, kindly man of about sixty. He guided us graciously through the unfamiliar menu and introduced us to the local delicacy, namely Nanjing Duck. This turned out to be very similar to Peking Duck (or Beijing Duck, as we now know it—or, to be strictly accurate, Szechwan Duck,

which is what we have been eating for years under the name Peking Duck. We had some wonderful Szechwan Duck in Beijing, because that's what they eat there. Beijing Duck is something different and comes in two courses, the second of which is usually not worth bothering with). To conclude: Nanjing Duck turned out to be very similar to Szechwan Duck except that they spoil the thing by coating it with a solid half-inch layer of salt. Professor Zhou agreed that it didn't taste nearly as pleasant that way, but that was how they did it in Nanjing.

Professor Zhou welcomed us to China, was surprised and delighted that we had come all this way to see the dolphins, said that he would do everything he possibly could to help us, but didn't think it would do us any good. Things are difficult in China, he confided. He promised to try and phone the people at the dolphin conservation project in Tongling to warn them that we were coming, but didn't hold out much hope of reaching them because he'd been trying to get through to them on his own account for weeks.

He said that, yes, we were right. The noise in the Yangtze was a major problem for the dolphins, and severely interfered with their echolocation. When the dolphins heard a boat, their habit had always been to make a long dive, change direction underwater, swim under the boat, and surface behind it. Now, when they are under the boat, they get confused and surface too soon, right under the propellers.

These things had all happened very suddenly, he said. The Yangtze had remained unspoiled for millions of years, but over the last few years had changed very dramatically, and the dolphin had no habit of adaptation.

The very existence of the dolphin had not been known of until relatively recently. Fishermen had always known of them, but fishermen did not often talk to zoologists, and there had been a recent painful period in China's history, of course, when nobody talked to scientists of any kind, merely denounced them to the Party for wearing glasses.

The dolphin was first discovered, in Dong Ting Lake, not in the Yangtze, in 1914 when a visiting American killed one and took it back to the Smithsonian. It was obviously a new species and genus of river dolphin, but little further interest was taken in it.

Then, in the late Fifties, Professor Zhou returned from a field trip studying birds, to find an unlabeled skeleton waiting for him. It was the same species of dolphin, but this had been discovered, not in Dong Ting Lake, where they no longer existed, but in the river near Nanjing.

He interviewed some local fishermen who said they did see them from time to time. Any that were accidentally caught were sold for food. The ones that got caught in the fishing lines had a bad time of it, because the lines the fishermen traditionally use along the banks of the Yangtze are baited with hundreds of large, bare hooks.

Some studies were carried out around Nanjing, but for a while the Cultural Revolution put a stop to all that. Research picked up again in the Seventies, but the difficulties of communication within China were such that research was only local, and no one really had a feel for exactly how rare the animal was, or what kind of predicament it was in.

That all changed in 1984.

Some peasants found a baiji stranded in the shallows near Tongling, further upriver. They reported it to the Agricultural Commission of the Tongling Municipal Government, who took an interest and sent someone along to take a look at it.

This immediately began to flush out a whole lot of stuff.

All sorts of people were suddenly popping up and saying that they had also seen a dolphin hit by a boat or caught in a net or washed up in a bloody mess somewhere.

The picture that emerged from putting all these hitherto isolated incidents together was an alarming one. It was suddenly horribly apparent that this dolphin was not merely rare, it was in mortal danger.

Professor Zhou was brought along from Nanjing to assess what should be done. Here the story took an unusual and dramatic turn, because once he had assessed what should be done . . . the people of Tongling did it.

Within months a huge project was set up to build a dolphin protection reserve within the Yangtze itself, and now, five years later, it is almost complete.

"You should go to see it," said Professor Zhou. "It is very good. I will try my best to phone them to prepare for your arrival, so you may rest . . . what is the word?"

I said that rest sounded fine to me. I was all for some rest.

"Easily? Surely? Ah . . . assured. You may rest assured that they will not be expecting you. So I will give you a letter also."

For various reasons which had to do with making a diversion to see an alligator farm from which we then got chased by police on the grounds that we did not have the appropriate alligator permits, we ended up taking a taxi to Tongling, a mere one hundred and twenty miles. We got a special deal on the taxi. Part of the special deal was that we didn't have a very good taxi driver, or indeed a very good taxi, and we arrived in Tongling in a state of some nervous tension.

Foreigners are not allowed to drive in China, and you can see why. The Chinese drive, or cycle, according to laws that are simply not apparent to an uninitiated observer, and I'm thinking not merely of the laws of the Highway Code, I'm thinking of the laws of physics. By the end of our stay in China, I had learned to accept that if you are driving along a two-lane road behind another car or truck, and there are two vehicles speeding toward you, one of which is overtaking the other, the immediate response of your driver will be to also pull out and overtake. Somehow, magically, it all works out in the end.

What I could never get used to, however, was this situation: the vehicle in front of you is overtaking the vehicle in

front of him, and your driver pulls out and *overtakes the overtaking vehicle,* just as three other vehicles are coming toward you performing exactly the same maneuver. Presumably Sir Isaac Newton has long ago been discredited as a bourgeois capitalist running-dog lackey.

Tongling, in turn, made us long wistfully for the cheerful, familiar hominess of Nanjing.

To quote the welcoming brochure for tourists that I found in my bleak hotel bedroom: "As a new rising industrial mining city, Tongling has already founded a rather [sic] scale of non-ferrous metallurgical, chemical, textile, building material, electronics, machinery, iron and steel and coal industries; especially the non-ferrous metallurgical building material and chemical industries, which, with a broad prospect of development, have already made or been on the way of making Tongling the major production centre."

Tongling was not beautiful. It was a bleak, grey, unwelcoming place, and I made immediate plans to lay down a territorial aftershave marker here.

168
▼▼▼

I took the brochure with me and met Mark and Chris in the hotel restaurant, which was also bleak. We had been pretty open to suggestion as far as food had been concerned in China, and had been prepared, sometimes recklessly prepared, to eat whatever people put in front of us. Much of it had been delicious, much of it less so, and some of it had been rather startling to a Western palate.

The food in this hotel fell heavily into the startling category, including, and especially, the Thousand-Year-Old eggs. The name is, of course, not meant to be taken literally, but merely as a sort of hint as to how startling they are.

The eggs are lightly boiled in green tea and then buried in a box of mud and straw for three months. In that time the white turns bright green and firm, and the yolk turns very, very dark green indeed and sludgy. The startling thing is that they are then presented to you as a delicacy, whereas if you

found them in your cupboard at home, you would call in the Sanitation Department.

We struggled a little with the meal, finally gave up, and looked through the brochure again, in which I discovered another passage: "It has been already decided to set up a water reserve to protect *Lipotes vexillifer,* a kind of precious rare mammal in Yangtze River, which is now regarded as 'Panda in water.'"

"Have you noticed the beer you're drinking?" Mark asked me.

I looked at the bottle. It was called Baiji Beer. It had a picture of a dolphin on the label, and the Latin name for it, *Lipotes vexillifer,* printed on the cap.

"I noticed another hotel on the way into town this afternoon," said Chris. "I thought, there's a funny coincidence, it's called the Baiji Hotel. Looked a sight better than this dump."

Even if we'd come to the wrong hotel, we'd clearly come to the right place.

169
▼▼▼

A day passed before, with the aid of Professor Zhou's letter, we were able to find an English-speaking guide and organise a small boat to go out onto the river and do what we had come to do: go out onto the Yangtze River and look for baiji dolphins ourselves.

We were by this time two or three days behind the schedule we had originally planned, and had to leave the following morning on a ferry to Wuhan. We had therefore only a few hours in which to try and see one of the rarest aquatic mammals in the world in a river in which it would be hard to see your hand in front of your face.

Our small boat chugged away from a small, crowded wharf and out onto a wide extent of the dirty brown river. We asked Mr. Ho, our guide, what he thought our chances of success were.

He shrugged.

"You see, there are only two hundred baiji in a hundred and twenty-five miles. And the Yangtze is very wide. Not good, I think."

We chugged along for quite some time, making our way gradually toward the opposite bank, about a mile away. The water was shallower there, which meant that there was less boat traffic. The dolphins also tend to keep close to the banks for the same reason, which means they are more likely to get snared in the fishing nets, of which we passed several, hung from bamboo frames extending from the banks. Fish populations are declining in the Yangtze and, with all the noise, the dolphins have greater difficulty in "seeing" the fish that there are. I guessed that a net full of fish might well lure a dolphin into danger.

We reached a relatively quiet spot near the bank, and the captain turned off the engine.

Mr. Ho explained that this was a good place to wait, maybe. Dolphins had been seen there recently. He said that that might be a good thing, or it might not. Either they would be here because they had been recently, or they would not be here because they had been recently. This seemed comfortably to cover all the options, so we sat quietly to wait.

The vastness of the Yangtze becomes very apparent when you try and keep a careful watch on it. Which bit of it? Where? It stretched endlessly ahead of us, behind us, and to one side. There was a breeze blowing, ruffling and chopping up the surface, and after just a few minutes of watching, your eyes begin to wobble. Every momentary black shadow of a dancing wave looks for an instant like what you want it to look like, and I did not even have a good mental picture of what to look for.

"Do you know how long they surface for?" I asked Mark.

"Yes . . ."

"And?"

"It isn't good news. The dolphin's melon, or forehead,

breaks the surface first, as it blows, then its small dorsal fin comes up, and then it plunges down again."

"How long does that take?"

"Less than a second."

"Oh." I digested this. "I don't think we're going to see one, are we?"

Mark looked depressed. With a sigh, he opened a bottle of Baiji Beer and took a rather complicated swig at it, so as not to take his eyes off the water.

"Well, we might at least see a finless porpoise," he said.

"They're not as rare as the dolphins, are they?"

"Well, they're certainly endangered in the Yangtze. There are thought to be about four hundred of them. They're having the same problems here, but you'll also find them in the coastal waters off China and as far west as Pakistan, so they're not in such absolute danger as a species. They can see much better than the baiji, which suggests that they're probably relative newcomers. Look! There's one! Finless porpoise!"

I was just in time to see a black shape fall back in the water and disappear. It was gone.

"Finless porpoise!" Mr. Ho called out to us. "You see?"

"We saw, thanks!" said Mark.

"How did you know it was a finless porpoise?" I asked, quite impressed by this.

"Well, two things, really. First, we could actually see it. It came right up out of the water. Finless porpoises do that. The baiji doesn't."

"You mean, if you can actually get to see it, it must be a finless porpoise?"

"More or less."

"What's the other reason?"

"Well, it didn't have a fin."

An hour drifted by. A couple of hundred yards from us, big cargo boats and barges growled up the river. A slick of

171
▼▼▼

oil drifted past. Behind us the fishnets fluttered in the wind. I thought to myself that the words "endangered species" had become a phrase that had lost any vivid meaning. We hear it too often to be able to react to it afresh.

As I watched the wind ruffling over the bilious surface of the Yangtze, I realised with the vividness of shock that somewhere beneath or around me there were intelligent animals whose perceptive universe we could scarcely begin to imagine, living in a seething, poisoned, deafening world, and that their lives were probably passed in continual bewilderment, hunger, pain, and fear.

We did not manage to see a dolphin in the wild. We knew that we would at least be able to see the only one that is held in captivity, in the Hydrobiology Institute in Wuhan, but nevertheless we were depressed and disappointed when we arrived back at our hotel in the early evening.

Here we suddenly discovered that Professor Zhou had managed to alert people to our arrival after all, and we were astonished to be greeted by a delegation of about a dozen officials from the Tongling Baiji Conservation Committee of the Tongling Municipal Government.

A little dazed by this unexpectedly formal attention when we'd just been going to slump over a beer, we were ushered in to a large meeting room in the hotel and shown to a long table. A little apprehensively, we sat on one side along with an interpreter whom they had provided for the occasion, and the members of the committee carefully arranged themselves along the other.

They sat quietly for a moment, each with their hands neatly folded on top of each other on the table in front of them, and looked distantly at us. My head swam for a moment with the hallucination that we were about to be arraigned before an ideological tribunal, before I realised that the distant formality of their manner probably meant that they were at least as shy of us as we were of them.

One or two of them were wearing a type of grey uniform tunic, one was wearing the old Maoist blue tunic, others were more casually dressed. They ranged in age from about mid-twenties to mid-sixties.

"The committee welcomes you to Tongling," began the interpreter, "and is honoured by your visit." He introduced them one by one, each in turn nodding to us with a slightly nervous smile. One was the Conservation Vice-Chief, another the Association Chief-Secretary, another the Vice Chief-Secretary, and so on.

I sat there feeling that we were stuck in the middle of some gigantic misunderstanding about something, and tried desperately to think of some way of looking intelligent and not letting on that I was merely a science-fiction comedy novelist on holiday.

Mark, however, seemed perfectly at ease. He explained simply and concisely who we were, leaving out the science-fiction comedy bit, outlined the nature of our project, said why we were interested in the baiji, and asked them an intelligent opening question about the reserve they were building.

I relaxed. I realised, of course, that talking intelligently about conservation projects to large committees in languages he didn't know was part of what he did for a living.

They explained to us that the dolphin reserve was what they called a "semi-nature reserve." Its purpose was to constrain the animals within a protected area without taking them out of their natural environment.

A little upstream of Tongling, opposite the town of Datong, there is an elbow-shaped bend in the river. In the crook of the elbow lie two triangular islands, between which runs a channel of water. The channel is about one and a half kilometres long, five metres deep, and between forty and two hundred metres wide, and this channel will be the dolphins' semi-nature reserve.

Fences of bamboo and metal are being constructed at either end of the channel, through which water from the main river flows continuously. A huge amount of remodeling and construction work is being done to make this possible. A large artificial hospital and holding pools are being built on one of the islands to hold injured or newly captured dolphins. A fish farm is being built on the other to feed them.

The scale of the project is enormous.

It is very, very expensive, the committee said solemnly, and they can't even be sure that it will work. But they have to try. The baiji, they explained, is very important to them and it is their duty to protect it.

Mark asked them how on earth they had raised the money to do it. It had all been put into operation in an extraordinarily short time.

Yes, they said, we have had to work very, very fast.

They had raised money from many sources. A substantial amount came from the central government, and more again from local government. Then there were many donations from local people and businesses.

They had also, they said a little hesitantly, gone into the business of public relations, and they would welcome our comments on this. Chinese knew little of such matters, but we, as Westerners, must surely be experts.

First, they said, they had persuaded the local brewery to use the baiji as their trademark. Had we tried Baiji Beer? It was of a good quality, now much respected in all of China. Then others had followed. The committee had entered into . . .

Here there was a bit of a vocabulary problem, which necessitated a little discussion with the interpreter before the right phrase at last emerged.

They had entered into licensing agreements. Local businesses had put money into the project, in return for which they were licensed to use the baiji symbol, which in turn made good publicity for the baiji dolphin.

So now there was not only Baiji Beer, there was also the

Baiji Hotel, Baiji shoes, Baiji Cola, Baiji computerised weigh-
ing scales, Baiji toilet paper, Baiji phosphorus fertiliser, and
Baiji Bentonite.

Bentonite was a new one for me, and I asked them what
it was.

They explained that Bentonite was a mining product used
in the production of toothpaste, iron and steel casting, and
also as an additive for pig food. Baiji Bentonite was a very
successful product. Did we, as experts, think that this public
relations was good?

We said it was absolutely astonishing, and congratulated
them.

They were very gratified to know this, they said, from
Western experts in such matters.

We felt more than a little abashed at these encomiums. It
was very hard to imagine anywhere in the Western world
that would be capable of responding with such prodigious
speed, imagination, and communal determination to such a
problem. Although the committee told us that they hoped
that, since Tongling had recently been declared an open city
to visitors for the first time, the dolphins and the semi-nature
reserve might bring tourists and tourist money to the area, it
was very clear that this was not the primary impulse.

At the end of our meeting they said, "The residents in the
area gain some profit—that's natural—but we have more
profound plans, that is to protect the dolphin as a species,
not to let it become extinct in our generation. Its protection
is our duty. As we know that only two hundred pieces of this
animal survive, it may go extinct if we don't take measures
to prevent it, and if that happens we will feel guilty for our
descendants and later generations."

We left the room feeling, for the first time in China,
uplifted. It seemed that, for all the stilted and awkward formality of the meeting, we had had our first and only real
glimpse of the Chinese mind. They took it as their natural

175
▼▼▼

duty to protect this animal, both for its own sake and for that of the future world. It was the first time we had been able to see beyond our own assumptions and have some insight into theirs.

I ordered the Thousand-Year-Old eggs again that night, determined to try to enjoy them.

RARE, OR
MEDIUM
RARE?

 ICHARD LEWIS
is a man who has worked out a foolproof way of getting
snappy answers to his questions.

He drives his Landrover (well, not actually *his* Landrover,
but the Landrover of anyone foolhardy enough to lend him
one) with what can only be described as pizzazz along Mauritian roads that were built with something less than pizzazz
in mind. The roads are often narrow and windy, and where
they are tarmacked, the tarmac tends to finish with an abrupt
six-inch drop at the edge. Richard drives along these with a
pizzazz that borders dangerously on élan, and when he asks
you a question, he turns and looks at you and doesn't look
back at the road again until you've answered. Mortal terror
is not the best state of mind in which to try and frame intelligent answers, but you have to try.

We had managed okay with "How was the flight?" ("Fine!") and "How was the meal?" ("Fine!") and "Feeling jet-lagged?" ("We're *fine!*"), but then we got to what he clearly regarded as being the crunch, so to speak.

"Why are you coming all the way to Mauritius to look for some crappy old *fruit bat?*" The Landrover veered frighteningly.

One of the first things you need to know about Richard Lewis, indeed *the* thing you need to know about him, is that he's an ornithologist. Once you know that, everything else more or less falls into place.

"I just couldn't figure it out," he protested, twisted halfway around in his seat to harangue us. "You're going to *Rodrigues?* To look for a *fruit bat?* It's not even particularly rare."

"Well, it's all relative," protested Mark. "It may not be particularly rare by Mauritian standards, but it is the rarest fruit bat in the—"

"Why don't you stay here on Mauritius, for heaven's sake?"

"Well . . ."

"What do you know about Mauritius? Anything?"

"Well," I said, "I know that . . . er, there's a lorry coming . . ."

"Never mind about that. I'll take care of the lorries. What do you know about Mauritius?"

"I know that it was originally colonised by the Dutch," I said. "And when they left, it was taken over by the French, who lost it to Britain after the Napoleonic Wars. So it's an ex-British colony, part of the Commonwealth. The inhabitants speak French or Creole. The law is basically English and you're, er, supposed to drive on the left—"

"All right, you've read the guide book. But do you know about the *birds* here? Don't you know about the pink pigeon? The echo parakeet? Don't you know about the Mauritius *kestrel?*"

"Yes, but . . ."

"Then why are you going off to the stupid island of Rodrigues to look for some ridiculous fruit bat? We've got a bunch of them here at the captive breeding centre if you really want to see one. Common as muck, stupid things. You'd be much better off staying here and seeing some *real* stuff. *Jesus!*"

He had suddenly caught an inadvertent glimpse of the road ahead of us and had to yank hard on the steering wheel to avoid an oncoming truck.

"Tell you what," he said, turning around again. "How long have you got? Two weeks?"

"Yes," said Mark hurriedly.

"And you were planning to spend two days here and then fly to Rodrigues to spend, what, ten days searching for the world's rarest fruit bat?"

"Yes."

"Okay. Here's what you do instead. You stay here for ten days, and then go off to Rodrigues for two days. Right?"

"Will we find it in two days?"

"Yes."

"How do you know?"

"Because I'll tell you exactly where to find it. Take you ten minutes. Take a couple of photos, go home."

"Oh."

"So you're staying here, right?"

"Er . . ."

We were swaying erratically along, more or less in the middle of the road. Another truck hove into sight ahead of us, frantically flashing its lights. Richard was still looking around at us.

"Agreed?" he insisted. "You'll stay?"

"Yes! Yes! We'll stay!"

"Right. Good. I should think so too. You'll get to meet Carl then as well. He's brilliant, but completely mad. *Jesus!*"

▼▼▼▼▼

The brilliant but completely mad Carl Jones is a tall Welsh-man in his late thirties, and there are those who say of him that his sheer perverse bloody-mindedness is the major thing that stands in the way of the almost total destruction of the ecology of Mauritius. It was Carl whom Mark had contacted to make the arrangements for our trip, and it had been quite apparent from the first moment that we set foot on Mauritius that he was a man to contend with. When we told the immigration official at the airport that we would be staying "with someone called Carl Jones at somewhere called Black River," it had produced the unexpected and unnerving response of hysterical laughter, and also a friendly pat on the back.

When Carl met us at Richard's house, he greeted us with a scowl, leaned against the doorframe, and growled, "I hate media people." Then he noticed our tape recorder and suddenly grinned impishly.

"Oh! Is that on?" he asked.

"Not at the moment."

180
▼▼▼

"Turn it on, quick, turn it on!"

We turned it on.

"I really *hate* media people!" he boomed at it. "Did you get that? Do you think it'll come out all right?"

He peered at the recorder to make sure the tape really was running.

"You know, I once did an interview for *Woman's Hour* on the radio," he said, shaking his head in wonderment at the folly of a malign and silly world. "I hate media people, they take up all my time and don't pay me very much—but anyway, the interviewer said to me that he was sick of boring scientists and could I tell him about my work but be sure to mention women and babies. So I told him that I preferred women field assistants to men, that we reared lots of baby birds, and that women were better at looking after baby birds because they were more sensitive and all that. And it went *out!*"

This rendered him speechless with laughter and he tottered helplessly out of the room and was not seen again for hours.

"That was Carl," said Richard. "He's great. He's really brilliant. Honestly. Don't worry about him being a complete sod."

We quickly discovered that we had fallen in with a bunch of passionately obsessed people. The first obsession for Carl and for Richard was birds. They loved them with an extraordinary fervour, and had devoted their entire adult lives to working in the field, often in awful conditions and on horribly low budgets, to save rare birds, and the environments they live in, from extinction. Richard had trained in the Philippines, working to save the Philippines' monkey-eating eagle, a wildly improbable-looking piece of flying hardware that you would more readily expect to see coming into land on an aircraft carrier than nesting in a tree. From there he had, in 1985, come to Mauritius, where the entire ecology of an island formerly famous for its abundant beauty is in desperate trouble.

181
▼▼▼

They work with a desperate energy that is disconcerting for a while until you begin to appreciate the enormity of the problems facing them, and the speed with which those problems are escalating. Ecologically speaking, Mauritius is a war zone and Carl, Richard, and others—including Wendy Strahm, an equally obsessed botanist—are like surgeons working just behind the front line. They are immensely kind people, often exhausted by the demands that their caring makes on them. Their impatience often erupts into a kind of wild black humour because, faced with so much that is absolutely critical, they can't afford the time for anything that is merely very, very urgent.

The focus of their work is Carl's captive breeding centre in the village of Black River, and Richard took us along to see it the next day.

We screeched to a halt outside the gate set in a six-foot-high stone wall and went in.

Inside was a large sandy courtyard, ringed with low wooden buildings, large aviaries, and cages. The warm air was rich with the sounds of flapping and cooing and sharp, bracing smells. Several very, very large tortoises were roaming about the centre of the yard completely free, presumably because virtually anybody would be able to beat them to the gate if they suddenly decided to make a break for it.

"There you are," said Richard, pointing at a large cage off to one side in which someone appeared to have hung a number of small broken umbrellas, "Rodrigues fruit bats. You can relax now, you've seen 'em. Look at them later, they're boring. They're nothing to what else we've got here. Pink pigeons for a start . . . this place has got some of the rarest, sexiest birds in the world. And you want to see the real stars? I'll see if Carl's in. He should be the one to show you."

He took us for a quick hunt, but Carl wasn't there. There was, however, someone who was besottedly in love with him. Richard beckoned us in.

"This is Pink," he said.

We looked.

Pink gazed at us intently with his two large, deep brown eyes. He fidgeted a little with his feet, clawing at his perch, and seemed tense, expectant, and slightly irritated to see us.

"Pink's a Mauritius kestrel," said Richard, "but he's basically weird."

"Really?" said Mark. "Doesn't look it."

"What does he look like to you?"

"Well, he's quite small. He's got sleek brown outer plumage on his wings, mottled brown and white breast feathers, impressive set of talons . . ."

"In other words, you think he looks like a bird."

"Well, yes . . ."

"He'd be shocked to know you thought that."

"What do you mean?"

"Well, one of the problems with breeding birds in captivity is that they sometimes have to be reared by humans, which leads to all sorts of misunderstandings on the bird's part. When a bird hatches from its egg, it doesn't have much of a clear picture of what's what in the world, and it falls in love with the first thing that feeds it, which in Pink's case was Carl. It's called 'imprinting,' and it's a major problem because you can't undo it. Once he's made up his mind that he's human, he—"

"He actually thinks he's a human?" I asked.

"Oh yes. Well, if he thinks Carl's his mother, it more or less follows, doesn't it? They may not be brilliant, but they're logical. He's quite convinced he's a human. He completely ignores the other kestrels, hasn't got time for them, they're just a bunch of birds as far as he's concerned. But when Carl walks in here he goes completely berserk. It's a problem because, of course, you can't introduce an imprinted bird into the wild, it wouldn't know what the hell to do. Wouldn't nest, wouldn't hunt, it would just expect to go to restaurants and stuff. Or at least it would expect to be fed. It wouldn't survive by itself.

"However, he does have a very important function in the aviary. You see, the young birds that we've hatched here don't come to sexual maturity at the same time, so when the females start getting sexy, the males are not ready to handle it. The females are bigger and more belligerent and often beat the males up. So when that happens, we collect semen from Pink, and—"

"How do you do that?" asked Mark.

"In a hat."

"I thought you said in a hat."

"That's right. Carl puts on this special hat, which is a bit like a rather strange bowler hat with a rubber brim, Pink goes mad with desire for Carl, flies down and fucks the hell out of his hat."

"What?"

183
▼▼▼

"He ejaculates into the brim. We collect the drop of semen and use it to inseminate a female."

"Strange way to treat your mother."

"He's a strange bird. But he does serve a useful purpose in spite of being psychologically twisted."

Setting up the captive breeding centre on Mauritius is one of Carl's major failures. In fact, it is the result of probably the most spectacular and brilliant failure of his life.

"They always thought I would be a failure when I was a boy," he told us when he turned up later, incredibly late for something. "I was hopeless, a complete write-off. Never did any work, wasn't interested in anything at all. Well, anything other than animals. Nobody at my school in Wales thought it was very useful being only interested in animals, but I had about fifty of them, to my father's despair, in cages all over the backyard. Badgers and foxes, wild Welsh polecats, owls, hawks, macaws, jackdaws, everything. I even managed, just as a schoolboy, to breed kestrels in captivity.

"My headmaster said it was nice that I had an interest, but I would never get anywhere because I was a lousy scholar. One day he called me into his study and said, 'Jones,' he said, 'this just isn't acceptable. You spend your whole life going around looking under hedges. You spend no time doing your schoolwork. You're a failure. What are you going to do with yourself?'

"I said—and remember, this was in Wales—'Sir, I want to go to tropical islands and study birds.'

"He said, 'But to do that you have to be either rich or intelligent and you're neither.'

"I took this as some kind of encouragement, finally managed to pass a few exams, went to college, and when I was an undergraduate I went to a lecture in Oxford by Professor Tom Cade, who's a world authority on falcons. He told us how in America they were working with peregrine falcons by breeding them in captivity and releasing the young back into the wild.

"I couldn't believe it. This was incredibly exciting. Here were these people going out and actually *doing* something. Then he said that in the Indian Ocean on an island called Mauritius there was a very rare bird, perhaps the rarest of all falcons, called the Mauritius kestrel, which was, at the moment, doomed to extinction, but that it could possibly be saved by captive breeding. And it suddenly came to me that all this work I'd been doing in my backyard as a kid, fiddling around with birds, could actually be used to save a whole species from becoming extinct.

"I was overwhelmed by excitement, and I thought, Christ, I must see if I can do something about this. So in the summer I went to America and studied a number of the projects there, saw how they were doing it, and promised myself that if I possibly could, I'd go to Mauritius and work to save the Mauritius kestrel.

"And they said, 'Well, Carl, it's all very well you wanting to go to Mauritius, but there's lots of problems out there and you can't save these birds. There just aren't enough of them. Just one breeding pair and a couple of other individuals. And with all the local problems and no facilities, it just can't be done. There's a small project there, but it's got to be closed down. It's just throwing good resources after bad.'

"But I got the job. The job was to close the project down. That was the job I came here to do, ten years ago, close the whole thing down, what there was of it. None of this was even here then," he said, looking around at the captive breeding centre in which they had raised more than forty Mauritius kestrels for gradual reintroduction to the wild, two hundred pink pigeons, and even a hundred Rodrigues fruit bats. "I suppose I have to admit," he said with a naughty smile, "that I've been a complete failure."

As he finished his story, his hand dropped to his knee and

he happened to catch sight of his watch. Instantly a distraught expression came over his face and he jumped to his
feet, clapping his hand to his head. He was late for a fund-
raising meeting.

We heard him complain regularly and bitterly, during our
time on Mauritius, that he was no good at administration or
politics, and yet to keep his work going he had to spend an
awful lot of time doing both. He constantly had to work
raising money, justifying and accounting for the money he
gets to the people he gets it from, and negotiating with the
various international conservation bodies who seem to watch
over his shoulder all the time. As far as he's concerned, all of
this just prevents him from doing the work he's best able to
do, and he wishes they'd leave him alone and let him get on
with it. Or rather, give him the money and then leave him
alone and let him get on with it. The whole project, to save
the fragile and unique ecology of Mauritius, is run on a
pathetically meagre budget, and money—or the lack of it—

186
▼▼▼

is the bane of Carl's life. He left in a harassed fluster.

"You'd think that everyone involved in conservation work
would be on the same side," said Mark after he'd gone, "but
there's just as much squabbling and bureaucracy as there is
in anything else."

"You're telling me," said Richard. "And it's always the
workers out in the field who get mucked about by it. Look
at these rabbits."

With a contemptuous wave of his hand, he showed us a
cage in which a few perfectly ordinary-looking rabbits sat
twitching at us.

"There's an island near here—a very, very important island as far as wildlife is concerned—called Round Island.
There are more unique species of plants and animals on
Round Island than there are on any equivalent area on earth.
About a hundred, hundred and fifty years ago, somebody
had the bright idea of introducing rabbits and goats to the
island so if anybody got shipwrecked there, they'd have

something to eat. The populations quickly got out of hand and it wasn't until the mid-Seventies that they managed to get rid of the goats. Then just a few years ago a team from New Zealand came to exterminate the rabbits, until someone realised that they were exterminating a rare breed of French rabbit that didn't exist anymore in Europe and it should therefore be transferred to mainland Mauritius and preserved in some way, i.e., by us.

"As far as I'm concerned," continued Richard, "we could just put them in the pot. They're just ordinary rabbits. Also, someone has come along since then and said, 'That's a load of rubbish—these aren't that particular variety.'

"So we've just got to sit here feeding these rabbits until the rabbit experts have decided whether they're valuable or not. It's a waste of our time and resources. I mean, just feeding all these animals is a problem. They all need something different and you have to work out what it is.

"These Rodrigues fruit bats you've come to see, we have to feed them on a mixture of fruit and powdered dog food reconstituted with milk. They used to be fed a diet rich in banana, which did them no good at all and only gave them a nervous tic." He shrugged.

"I don't know what you've got against them," said Mark. "I think they're great animals."

"I've nothing against them. They're great. They're just common, that's all."

Mark protested, "It's the rarest fruit bat in—"

"Yeah, but there are *hundreds* of them," insisted Richard.

"Hundreds means they're severely endangered!" said Mark.

"Do you know how many echo parakeets there are in the wild?" exclaimed Richard. "Fifteen! *That's* rare. Hundreds is common. When you come to Mauritius and you see things in such a last-ditch state, everything else becomes unimportant. It becomes unimportant because we're witnessing here a species which could be saved if people put their minds to

it, and if it does go extinct it will be our fault because we never got around to saving it. There's fifteen of them left. We've got the kestrels up and the pigeons up purely because of the effort we've put into them, the money and the personnel. The parakeets? We're working very, very hard to save them, and if we don't manage it, they will be gone forever, and we have to worry about somebody else's rabbits."

He shook his head, and then calmed down.

"Listen," he said to Mark. "You're right. The Rodrigues fruit bat is a very important animal, and we are working to protect it. It's lost a lot of its habitat because the people of Rodrigues live by subsistence farming, which means that they've done a lot of forest clearance. The bat population is so reduced that one big cyclone—and we get them here— could wipe them out. But the Rodriguans have suddenly realised that it's actually damaging their own interests to cut down the forest, because it's reducing their water supply. If they want to preserve their watersheds, they have to preserve the forests, which means the bats get somewhere to live. So they're in with a chance. By the world's standards, they're severely endangered, but by the standards of these islands where every indigenous species is endangered, they're doing fine."

He grinned. "Want to see some endangered mice?"

"I didn't think mice were an endangered species yet," I said.

"I didn't say anything about the species," said Richard. "I just meant the particular mice. Conservation is not for the squeamish. We have to kill a lot of animals, partly to protect the species that are endangered, and partly to feed them. A lot of the birds are fed on mice, so we have to breed them here."

He disappeared into a small, warm, squeaking room and reemerged a few seconds later with a handful of freshly killed mice.

"Time to feed the birds," he said, heading back toward the Landrover from hell.

The best and quickest road to the Black River gorges where the kestrels live is a private one through the Medine sugar estate.

Sugar, from the point of view of the ecology of Mauritius, is a major problem. Vast swathes of the Mauritius forest have been destroyed to provide space to grow a cash crop which in turn destroys our teeth. This is serious anywhere, but on an island it is a very special problem, because island ecologies are fundamentally different from mainland ones. They even have a different vocabulary. When you spend much time on islands with naturalists, you will tend to hear two words in particular an awful lot: *endemic* and *exotic*. Three, if you count *disaster*.

An endemic species of plant or animal is one that is native to an island or region and is found nowhere else at all. An exotic species is one that has been introduced from abroad, and a disaster is usually what results when this occurs.

The reason is this: continental land masses are big. They support hundreds of thousands, even millions, of different species, each of which are competing with one another for survival. The sheer ferocity of the competition for survival is immense, and it means that the species that do survive and flourish are mean little fighters. They grow faster and throw out a lot more seeds.

An island, on the other hand, is small. There are far fewer species, and the competition for survival has never reached anything like the pitch that it does on the mainland. Species are only as tough as they need to be, life is much quieter and more settled, and evolution proceeds at a much slower rate. This is why you find on Madagascar, for instance, species like the lemurs that were overwhelmed eons ago on the mainland. Island ecologies are fragile time capsules.

So you can imagine what happens when a mainland species gets introduced to an island. It would be like introducing Al Capone, Genghis Khan, and Rupert Murdoch into the Isle of Wight—the locals wouldn't stand a chance.

So what happens on Mauritius, or indeed any island, is that when endemic vegetation or animals are destroyed for any reason, the exotic forms leap into the breach and take over. It's hard for an Englishman to think of something like privet as being an exotic and ferocious life form—my grandmother has neatly trimmed privet bushes lining her front garden—but in Mauritius it behaves like a bunch of marauding triffids. So does the introduced guava and numerous other foreign invaders, which grow much more quickly and produce many more seeds.

Black ebony comes from the lowland hardwood forests of Mauritius, and is why the Dutch first colonised the island. There's hardly any of it left now. The reasons for the forest being cut down include straightforward logging and clearing space for cash crops. And another reason: deer hunting. Le Chasse.

Vast tracts of forest have been cleared to make room for game parks, in which hunters stand on short wooden towers and shoot at herds of deer that are driven past them. As if the original loss of the forest were not bad enough—and for such a reason—the grazing habits of the deer keep the fragile endemic plants from regrowing, while the exotic species thrive in their place. Young Mauritian trees are simply nibbled to death.

We passed through huge fields of swaying sugarcane, having first negotiated our way past the sugar estate's gatekeeper, an elderly and eccentric Mauritian named James who will not let anybody through his gate without a permit, even someone he's let through every day for ten years but who has accidentally left his permit at home that day. He did this to Carl recently, who since then has been threatening to Superglue the gate shut in revenge, and it's quite possible that he will. Carl is clearly the sort of person who will get as many laughs as he can from a situation by threatening to do something silly and then try and get a few more by actually doing it.

There had been a more serious confrontation a little while earlier when Carl and Wendy arrived with a party of officials from the World Bank from whom they were negotiating some financial support. James wouldn't let them in on the grounds that they had two cars and he was only authorised to let in one.

James also reports to Carl and Richard regularly about the movements of the kestrels, not because they've asked him to but just because, other evidence to the contrary, he likes to help. If he hasn't actually seen any kestrels, he'll still, in a friendly and encouraging sort of a way, say that he has. This means that now, whenever Carl has to change the coloured bands the kestrels wear around their legs, he makes a point of putting on a different colour so that he will know James is lying if he claims to have seen a kestrel with a band that doesn't exist.

The kestrel we were going to see had been trained to take mice in 1985. The purpose of feeding kestrels in the wild was to bump up their diet and encourage them to lay more eggs. If a kestrel was well fed, then Carl could take the first clutch of eggs the bird laid from its nest back to the breeding centre, confident that the kestrel would simply lay some more. In this way they were increasing the number of eggs that might hatch, but there was a limit to the number of birds available to sit on them, so they had to be incubated artificially. This is a highly skilled and delicate task and requires constant monitoring of the egg's condition. If an egg is losing weight too rapidly, by evaporation of liquid through the shell, then portions of the shell are sealed. If it is not losing enough, then portions of the shell are meticulously sanded to make it more porous. It is best if an egg can have one week under a real bird and the other three in the incubator—eggs that have

been swapped around like that have a much higher success rate.

Richard yanked the Landrover to a halt on the edge of the forest near the bottom of the gorge and we piled out of it. The air was brisk and clear, and Richard strode about the small clearing making an odd assortment of calling noises.

Within a minute or two the kestrel came zipping through the forest and perched itself up in a high tree overlooking a large hemispherical rock. Since the bird is adapted to living in the forest rather than the open land, it does not hover like many falcons, but can instead fly at great speeds unerringly through the forest canopy, where it catches its food of geckos, smaller birds, and insects. For this it relies on having fantastically keen and fast eyesight.

We watched it for a while and it watched us intently. In fact, it watched everything that moved, glancing rapidly in one direction after another with constant attention.

"See the way it's so interested in everything it can see?" said Richard. "It lives by its eyes, and you have to remember that when you keep them in captivity. You must make sure they have a complex environment. Birds of prey are comparatively stupid. But because they've got such incredible vision, you've got to have things that will keep them occupied visually.

"When we originally started breeding birds of prey in captivity, we brought in some very skittish birds, and whenever anybody went past the aviary the birds just went mad, and we thought they must be upset by the disturbance, and someone came up with the bright idea of what's called a skylight and seclusion aviary. All four walls were opaque and just the roof was open so that there was no disturbance for the birds. But what we found was that we'd overdone it. The offspring that were born in those environments were basket cases because they hadn't got the sensory input they needed. We'd got it completely the wrong way around.

"I mean, animals may not be intelligent, but they're not as stupid as a lot of human beings. You look at the primate areas in some zoos that are equipped with green metal architect-designed 'trees' that, in a minimalist sort of way, reproduce the shape of the tree, but don't actually include any of the features that a monkey might find interesting about a tree: leaves and bark and stuff. It may look like a tree to an architect, but architects are a lot more stupid than monkeys. We just got a brochure through from the States for exactly this—fibreglass trees. The whole brochure was designed to show us how proud they were of what they could sell us here in Mauritius, and showing the particular paints they had for *painting* lichen on trees. I mean, it's bloody ridiculous, who are these people? Okay. Let's feed the bird. You watching?"

The bird was watching. It's hard to avoid saying that it was watching like a hawk. It was watching like a kestrel.

Richard swung his arm back. The kestrel's head followed his movement precisely. With a wide underarm swing, Richard lobbed the small mouse high up into the air. For a second or so, the kestrel just watched it, jittering its legs very slightly on the branch as it engaged in monumental feats of differential calculus. The mouse reached the top of its steep parabola, its tiny dead weight turning slowly in the air.

At last the kestrel dropped from its perch and swung out into the air as if on the end of a long pendulum, the precise length, pivotal position, and swing speed of which the kestrel had calculated. The arc it described intersected sweetly with that of the falling mouse, the kestrel took the mouse cleanly into its talons, swept on up into another nearby tree, and bit its head off.

"He eats the head himself," said Richard, "and takes the rest of the mouse to the female in the nest."

We fed the kestrel a few more mice, sometimes throwing them in the air and sometimes leaving them on the hemispherical rock for it to dive for at its leisure. At last the bird was fed up and we left.

The term "fed up" actually comes from falconry. Most of the vocabulary of falconry comes from middle English, and zoologists have adopted a lot of it.

For instance, "feeking" describes the process by which the bird cleans its beak of meat after eating, by rubbing it along a branch. "Mutes" are the white trails along cliffs where the bird has been sitting. These are more normally called "bird droppings," of course, but in falconry talk they're "mutes." "Rousing" is the action of shaking its wings and body, which is generally a sign that the bird is feeling very comfortable and relaxed.

When you train a falcon, you train it by hunger, using it as a tool to manipulate the bird's psychology. So when the bird has had too much to eat, it won't cooperate and gets annoyed by any attempts to tell it what to do. It simply sits in the top of a tree and sulks. It is "fed up."

Richard became extremely fed up that evening, and with reason. It was nothing to do with eating too much, though it had a little to do with what other people liked to eat. A Mauritian friend came around to see him and brought her boss with her, a Frenchman from the nearby island of Réunion who was visiting the island for a few days and staying with her.

His name was Jacques, and we all took an instant dislike to him, but none so strongly as Richard, who detested him on sight.

He was a Frenchman of the dapper, arrogant type. He had lazy, supercilious eyes, a lazy, supercilious smile, and, as Richard later put it, a lazy, supercilious, and terminally stupid brain.

Jacques arrived at the house and stood around looking lazy and supercilious. He clearly did not quite know what he was doing in this house. It was not a very elegant house. It was full of battered, second-hand furniture, and had pictures of birds stuck all over the walls with drawing pins. He obviously wanted to slouch moodily against a wall, but could not find a wall that he was prepared to put his shoulder to, so he had to slouch moodily where he was standing.

We offered him a beer, and he took one with the best grace he could muster. He asked us what we were doing here, and we said we were taping a program for the BBC and writing a book about the wildlife of Mauritius.

"But why?" he said in a puzzled tone. "There is nothing here."

Richard showed admirable restraint at first. He explained quite coolly that some of the rarest birds in the world were to be found on Mauritius. He explained that that was what he and Carl and the others were there for: to protect and study and breed them.

Jacques shrugged and said that they weren't particularly interesting or special.

"Oh?" said Richard quietly.

"Nothing with any interesting plumage."

"Really?" said Richard.

"I prefer something like the Arabian cockatoo," said Jacques with a lazy smile.

"Do you."

"Me, I live on Réunion," said Jacques.

"Do you."

"There are certainly no interesting birds there," said Jacques.

"That's because the French have shot them all," said Richard.

He turned around smartly and went off into the kitchen to wash up, very, very loudly. Only when Jacques had gone did he return. He stalked back into the room carrying an unopened bottle of rum and slammed himself into the corner of a battered old sofa.

"About five years ago," he said, "we took twenty of the pink pigeons that we had bred at the centre and released them into the wild. I would estimate that in terms of the

195
▼▼▼

time, work, and resources we had put into them, they had
cost us about fifteen hundred dollars per bird. But that's not
the issue. The issue is holding on to the unique life of this
island. But within a short time all of those birds we had bred
were in casseroles. Couldn't believe it. We just couldn't believe it.

"Do you understand what's happening to this island? It's
a mess. It's a complete ruin. In the Fifties it was drenched
with DDT, which found its way straight into the food chain.
That killed off a lot of animals. Then the island was hit with
cyclones. Well, we can't help that, but they hit an island that
was already terribly weakened by all the DDT and logging,
so they did irreparable damage. Now with the continued
logging and burning of the forest, there's only ten percent
left, and they're cutting that down for deer hunting. What's
left of the unique species of Mauritius is being overrun by
stuff that you can find all over the world—privet, guava, all
this crap. Here, look at this."

196
▼▼▼

He handed the bottle to us. It was a locally brewed rum
called Green Island.

"Read what it says on the bottle."

Underneath a romantic picture of an old sailing ship approaching an idyllic tropical island was a quotation from
Mark Twain, which read, "You gather the idea that Mauritius was made first and then heaven; and that heaven was
copied after Mauritius."

"That was less than a hundred years ago," said Richard.
"Since then just about everything that shouldn't be done to
an island has been done to Mauritius. Except perhaps nu-
clear testing."

There is one island in the Indian Ocean, close to Mauritius,
which is miraculously unspoilt, and that is Round Island. In
fact, it isn't a miracle at all, there's a very simple reason for
it, which we discovered when we talked to Carl and Richard
about going there.

"You can't," said Carl. "Well, you can try, but I doubt if you'd manage it."

"Why not?" I asked.

"Waves. You know, the sea," said Carl. "Goes like this." He made big heaving motions with his arms.

"It's extremely difficult to get on," said Richard. "It has no beaches or harbours. You can only go there on very calm days, and even then you have to jump from the boat to the island. It's quite dangerous. You've got to judge it exactly right or you'll get thrown against the rocks. We haven't lost anybody yet, but . . ."

They almost lost me.

We hitched a ride on a boat trip with some naturalists going to Round Island, anchored about a hundred yards from the rocky coastline, and ferried ourselves across in a dinghy to the best thing that Round Island has to offer by way of a landing spot—a slippery outcrop called Pigeon House Rock.

A couple of men in wetsuits first leapt out of the dinghy into the tossing sea, swam to the rock, climbed with difficulty up the side of it, and at last slithered, panting, onto the top.

Everyone else in turn then made the trip across in the dinghy, three or four at a time. To land, you had to make the tricky jump across onto the rock, matching the crests of the incoming waves to the top of the rock, and leaping just an instant before the wave reached its height, so that the boat was still bearing you upward. Those already on the rock would be tugging at the dinghy's rope, shouting instructions and encouragement over the crashing of the waves, then catching and hauling people as they jumped.

I was to be the last one to land.

By this time the sea swell was getting heavier and rougher, and it was suggested that I should land on the other side of the rock, where it was a lot steeper but a little less obviously slippery with algae.

I tried it. I leapt from the edge of the heaving boat, lunged

for the rock, found it to be every bit as slippery as the other side, merely much steeper, and slithered gracelessly down it into the sea, grazing my legs and arms against the jagged edges. The sea closed over my head. I thrashed about under the surface, trying desperately to get my head up, but the dinghy was directly above me and kept bashing me against the rock face whenever I tried to make for the surface.

Okay, I thought, I've got the point. This is why the island is relatively unspoilt. I made one more lunge upward, just as those onshore succeeded at last in pushing the boat away from me. This allowed me to get my head up above water and cling on to a crack in the rock. With a lot more slipping and sliding and thrashing in the heavy swell, I managed finally to maneuver myself up to within arm's reach of Mark and the others, who yanked me urgently up and onto the rock. I sat in a spluttering, bleeding heap protesting that I was fine and all I needed was a quiet corner to go and die in and everything would be all right.

The sea had been swelling heavily for the two or three hours it had taken us to reach the island and it seemed as if my stomach had heaved something approaching my entire body weight into the sea, so by this time I was feeling pretty wobbly and strung out, and my day on Round Island passed in rather a blur. While Mark went with Wendy Strahm, the botanist, to try and find some of the species of plants and animals that exist only here on this single island, I went and sat in the sun near a palm tree called Beverly and felt dazed and sorry for myself.

I knew that the palm tree was called Beverly because Wendy told me that was what she had christened it. It was a bottle palm, so called because it is shaped like a Chianti bottle, and it was one of the eight that remain on Round Island, the only eight wild ones in the world.

Who on earth, I wondered as I sat next to Beverly in a sort of companionable gloom, gets to name the actual islands?

I mean, here was one of the most amazing islands in the

world. It looked utterly extraordinary, as if the moon itself was rising from the sea—except that where the moon would be cold and still, this was hot and darting with life. Though it appeared to be dusty and barren at first sight, the craters with which the surface was pocked were full of dazzling white-tailed tropic birds, brilliant Telfair's skinks, and Guenther's geckos.

You would think that if you had to come up with a name for an island like this, you'd invite a couple of friends over, get some wine, and make an evening of it. Not just say, "Oh, it's a little bit round, let's call it 'Round Island.' " Apart from anything else, it isn't even particularly round. There was another island just visible on the horizon, which was much more nearly round, but that is called Serpent Island, presumably to honour the fact that, unlike Round Island, it hasn't got any snakes on it. And there was yet another island I could see which sloped steadily from a peak at one end down to the sea at the other, and that, unaccountably, was called Flat Island. I began to see that whoever had named the islands probably had made a bit of an evening of it after all.

The reason that Round Island has remained a refuge for unique species of skinks, geckos, boas, palm trees, and even grasses that died out long ago on Mauritius is not simply that it is hard for man to get onto the island, but that it has proved completely impossible for rats to get ashore. Round Island is one of the largest tropical islands in the world (at a bit over three hundred acres) on which rats do not occur.

Not that Round Island is undamaged—far from it. A hundred and fifty years ago, before sailors introduced goats and rabbits onto the island, it was covered in hardwood forest, which the foreign animals destroyed. That is why from a distance and to the untutored eye, such as mine, the island appeared to be more or less barren at first sight. Only a naturalist would be able to tell you that the few odd-shaped palms and clumps of grass dotted about the place on the hot, dry, dusty land were unique and unspeakably precious.

199
▼▼▼

▼▼▼▼▼▼

Precious to whom? And why?

Does it actually matter very much to anyone other than a bunch of obsessed naturalists that the eight bottle palm trees on Round Island are the only ones to be found in the wild anywhere in the world? Or that the *Hyophorbe amaricaulis* (a palm tree so rare that it doesn't have any name other than its scientific one) standing in the Curepipe Botanic Gardens in Mauritius is the only one of its kind in existence? (The tree was only discovered by chance while the ground on which it stands was being cleared in order to construct the Botanic Gardens. It was about to be cut down.)

There is no "tropical island paradise" I know of that remotely matches up to the fantasy ideal that such a phrase is meant to conjure up, or even to what we find described in holiday brochures. It's natural to put this down to the discrepancy we are all used to finding between what advertisers promise and what the real world delivers. It doesn't surprise us much anymore.

So it can come as a shock to realise that the world we hear described by travelers of previous centuries (or even previous decades) and biologists of today really did exist. The state it's in now is only the result of what we've done to it, and the mildness of the disappointment we feel when we arrive somewhere and find that it's a bit tatty is only a measure of how far our own expectations have been degraded and how little we understand what we've lost. The people who do understand what we've lost are the ones who are rushing around in a frenzy trying to save the bits that are left.

The system of life on this planet is so astoundingly complex that it was a long time before man even realised that it was a system at all and that it wasn't something that was just there.

To understand how anything very complex works, or even to know that there is something complex at work, man needs to see little tiny bits of it at a time. And this is why small islands have been so important to our understanding of life. On the Galápagos Islands, for instance, animals and plants that shared the same ancestors began to change and adapt in different ways once they were divided from one another by a few miles of water. The islands neatly separated out the component parts of the process for us, and it was thus that Charles Darwin was able to make the observations that led directly to the idea of Evolution.

The island of Mauritius gave us an equally important but more sombre idea—extinction.

The most famous of all the animals on Mauritius is a large, gentle dove. A remarkably large dove, in fact: its weight is closest to that of a well-fed turkey. Its wings long ago gave up the idea of lifting such a plumpy off the ground and withered away into decorative little stumps. Once it gave up flying, it could adapt itself very well to the Mauritian seasonal cycle, and stuff itself silly in the late summer and autumn, when fruit is lying rich on the ground, and then live on its fat reserves, gradually losing weight, during the leaner, dry months.

It didn't need to fly anyway, since there were no predators that wished it any harm and it, in turn, is harmless itself. In fact, the whole idea of harm is something it has never learned to understand, so if you were to see one on the beach, it would be quite likely to walk right up to you and take a look, provided it could find a path through the armies of giant tortoises parading around the beach. There's never even been any reason for humans to kill it because its meat is tough and bitter.

It has a large, wide, downturned bill of yellow and green, which gives it a slightly glum and melancholic look, small, round eyes like diamonds, and three ridiculously little plumes sticking out of its tail. One of the first Englishmen to see this large dove said that "for shape and rareness, it might antagonise the Phoenix of Arabia."

None of us will ever see this bird, though, because, sadly,

201
▼▼▼

the last one was clubbed to death by Dutch colonists in about 1680.

The giant tortoises were eaten to extinction because the early sailors regarded them much as we regard canned food. They just picked them off the beach and put them on their ships as ballast, and then, if they felt hungry, they'd go down to the hold, pull one up, kill it, and eat it.

But the large, gentle dove—the dodo—was just clubbed to death for the sport of it. And that is what Mauritius is most famous for: the extinction of the dodo.

There had been extinctions before, but this was a particularly remarkable animal, and it only lived in the naturally limited area of the island of Mauritius. There were, very clearly and obviously, no more of them. And since only dodos could make a new dodo, there never would be any more of them ever again. The facts were very clearly and starkly delineated for us by the boundaries of the island.

Up until that point it hadn't really clicked with man that an animal could just cease to exist. It was as if we hadn't realised that if we kill something, it simply won't be there anymore. Ever. As a result of the extinction of the dodo, we are sadder and wiser.

We finally made it to Rodrigues, a small island dependency of Mauritius, to look for the world's rarest fruit bat, but first we went to look at something Wendy Strahm was very keen for us to see—so much so that she rearranged her regular Rodrigues-visiting schedule to take us there herself.

By the side of a hot and dusty road there was a single small bushy tree that looked as if it had been put in a concentration camp.

The plant was a kind of wild coffee called *Ramus mania*, and it had been believed to be totally extinct. Then, in 1981, a teacher from Mauritius named Raymond Aquis was teaching at a school in Rodrigues and gave his class pictures of about ten plants thought to be extinct on Mauritius.

One of the children put up his hand and said, "Please, sir, we've got this growing in our back garden."

At first it was hard to believe, but they took a branch of it and sent it to Kew, where it was identified. It was wild coffee.

The plant was standing by the side of the road, right by the traffic and in considerable danger because any plant in Rodrigues is considered fair game for firewood. So they put a fence around it to keep it from being cut down.

As soon as they did this, however, people started thinking, "Aha, this is a special plant," and they climbed over the fence and started to take off little branches and leaves and pieces of bark. Because the tree was obviously special, everybody wanted a piece of it and started to ascribe remarkable properties to it—it would, for example, cure hangovers and gonorrhea. Since not much goes on in Rodrigues other than home entertainments, it quickly became a very sought-after plant, and it was rapidly being killed by having bits cut off it.

The first fence was soon rendered useless and a barbed-wire fence was put around that. Then another barbed-wire fence had to be put around the first barbed-wire fence, and then a third barbed-wire fence had to be put around the second till the whole compound covered a half-acre. Then a guard was installed to watch the plant as well.

203
▼▼▼

With cuttings from this one plant, botanists at Kew Gardens are currently trying to root and cultivate two new plants, in the hope that it might then be possible to reintroduce them into the wild. Until they succeed, this single plant standing within its barbed-wire barricades will be the only representative of its species on earth, and it will continue to need protecting from everyone who is prepared to kill it in order to have a small piece. It's easy to think that as a result of the extinction of the dodo, we are now sadder and wiser, but there's a lot of evidence to suggest that we are merely sadder and better informed.

At dusk that day we stood by the side of another road,

where we had been told we would have a good view, and watched as the world's rarest fruit bats left their roost in the forest and flapped across the darkening sky to make their nightly forage among the fruit trees.

The bats are doing just fine. There are hundreds of them.

I have a terrible feeling that we are in trouble.

MARK'S EPILOGUE

AS THIS REALLY our last chance to see these animals? Unfortunately, there are too many unknowns for there to be a simple answer. With strenuous efforts in the field, the populations of some have actually begun to rise. But it is clear that if those efforts were suspended for a moment, the kakapos, the Yangtze river dolphins, the northern white rhinos, and many others would vanish almost immediately.

Not that a large population necessarily guarantees an animal's survival, as experience has shown many times in the past. The most famous example is the North American passenger pigeon, which was once the commonest bird that ever lived on earth. Yet it was hunted to extinction in little more than fifty years. We didn't learn any lessons from that experience: ten years ago, there were 1.3 million elephants in

Africa, but so many have been killed by poachers that today no more than 600,000 are left.

On the other hand, even the smallest populations can be brought back from the brink. Juan Fernandez fur seal numbers dropped from millions to fewer than one hundred by 1965; today, there are three thousand. And in New Zealand in 1978, the population of Chatham Island robins was down to one pregnant female, but the dedication of Don Merton and his team saved the species from extinction and there are now more than fifty.

The kakapo may also be on a slow road to recovery. Soon after we returned to England, we received the following letter from New Zealand:

P.O. Box 3
Stewart Island

Dear Douglas and Mark,

206
▼▼▼

I hope this reaches you quickly—I have some good news from kakapo country on southern Stewart Island. At 08.45 hrs on 25 August 1989 one of our dog handlers, Alan Munn, and his English setter 'Ari' located a new female kakapo near Lees Knob, at an altitude of 380 metres. 'Jane' weighed 1.25 kg and she scrarked a lot when Alan picked her up. She had just finished moulting but looked in good condition, so in a few days she will be flown to her new home—Codfish Island.

Once again, thanks very much for your visit. It certainly helped give those Big Green Budgies some of the attention they deserve.

Yours sincerely,
Andy Roberts (kakapo project manager)
for R. Tindal, District Conservator, Department of Conservation, Rakiura.

We later received some further good news about the kakapos. Two more females had been found on Stewart Island

and transferred to Codfish, bringing the total kakapo population up to forty-three.

Meanwhile, on Little Barrier Island, several of the males there have been booming for the first time, including, to everyone's delight, a nine-year-old called Snark. Born on Stewart Island in 1981, Snark was the only kakapo chick to have been seen by anyone this century.

But the best news of all was still to come. Just before going to press, a very excited Don Merton telephoned to say that a newly made kakapo nest had just been found on Little Barrier Island. Inside the nest, which was built by a nine-year-old female called Heather, was a single kakapo egg.

Transferring kakapos to Little Barrier and Codfish Islands has been a calculated risk—but it is the only hope of saving the kakapo from extinction. Heather's nest is the first encouraging sign that the project is actually working, and now everyone is waiting nervously to see if her egg will hatch and if she can raise the chick in her adopted home.

We also received a letter from Kes Hillman-Smith in Zaïre saying that three baby northern white rhinos have been born in Garamba since we left, bringing the total population up to twenty-five. The enthusiastic park staff have named them Mpiko, meaning "courage"; Molende, meaning "perseverance"; and Minzoto, meaning "a star."

It's important to recognise that not every conservation strategy necessarily works: we are often experimenting in the dark. During the early stages of the Garamba project, a lot of pressure was put on the Zaïrois to have all of their northern white rhinos captured and taken into captivity. The government of Zaïre would not agree to this. They said that the rhinos belong to them and they didn't want them to go to zoos in other parts of the world. Fortunately, it seems that this was the right decision. Northern white rhinos, it turned out, do not breed well in captivity—the last one was born in 1982—whereas more than ten have been born in the same period in the wild.

▼▼▼▼▼▼

The news from Mauritius has been more mixed. The kestrels are doing well and Carl believes that there could now be as many as a hundred of them in the wild, including twelve breeding pairs. However, the population of truly wild pink pigeons has dropped to fewer than ten. Some of the pigeons that have been bred in captivity are being released again. So far, they have escaped the hunters and appear to be doing well.

As for the echo parakeets, at least one of them has died since we saw them, though some of the others have been attempting to breed. In November 1989, Carl found a parakeet nest with three eggs inside. One of these mysteriously disappeared soon afterward, so he decided to risk removing the others to the captive breeding centre for safe-keeping. Both eggs hatched successfully and the chicks are fit and well.

Perhaps most important of all (for non-ornithologists), the wild population of Rodrigues fruit bats has just passed the one thousand mark.

208
▼▼▼

In contrast, after the BBC radio series had been broadcast, we received a disturbing letter from a couple who had been working in China:

(address supplied)

Dear Douglas and Mark,

We enjoyed the Yangtze dolphin programme—but listened with a touch of guilt! We recently spent three months working in a number of factories in Nanjing. We had a wonderful time with the people and ate well. To honour us when we left, one of them cooked a Yangtze dolphin, so really there should be 201. Sorry about that.

Yours,
(name supplied)

P.S. Sorry, it was two dolphins—my husband reminds me that he was guest of honour and had the embryo.

There is probably little hope of saving the dolphins in the Yangtze River itself, despite all the time and effort invested in protecting them. Perhaps in semi-captivity, in the reserve at Tongling and the new one at Shi Shou, they will stand a chance—though it could never be the same as being wild and free. Meanwhile, of course, the noise and pollution continue.

No one knows how many other species are this close to extinction. We don't even know how many species of animals and plants there are altogether in the world. A staggering 1.4 million have been found and identified so far, but some experts believe that there are another 30 million yet to be discovered. It's not surprising when you consider that we know more about the surface of the moon than we do about parts of our own planet. Many animals and plants are disappearing even before we are aware of their existence, perhaps hidden away somewhere in the depths of an unexplored sea or in a quiet corner of a tropical rain forest.

And it's not only the tiny, obscure creatures that have managed to escape our attention. There have been some exciting new discoveries in the rain forests of Madagascar, for example, since Douglas and I were there looking for the aye-aye in 1985. Field researchers have found two new species of lemur: one, called the golden bamboo lemur, has beautiful golden eyebrows, orange cheeks, and a rich reddish-brown coat; the other has a shock of golden orange on the top of its head and has been named the golden-crowned sifaka.

Both lemurs are extremely rare—and virtually unknown. What roles do they play in Madagascar's rain forests? Do they have any direct relevance to our own lives? What are the main threats to their survival? We don't know. They could become extinct before the experts learn enough to save them. Wildlife conservation is always a race against time. As

zoologists and botanists explore new areas, scrabbling to record the mere existence of species before they become extinct, it is like someone hurrying through a burning library desperately trying to jot down some of the titles of books that will now never be read.

Extinctions, of course, have been happening for millions of years: animals and plants were disappearing long before people arrived on the scene. But what has changed is the extinction *rate*. For millions of years, on average, one species became extinct every century. But most of the extinctions since prehistoric times have occurred in the last three hundred years.

And most of the extinctions that have occurred in the last three hundred years have occurred in the last fifty.

And most of the extinctions that have occurred in the last fifty have occurred in the last ten.

It is the sheer rate of acceleration that is as terrifying as anything else. There are now more than a thousand different species of animals and plants becoming extinct every year.

There are currently five billion human beings and our numbers are continually growing. We are fighting for space with the world's wildlife, which has to contend with hunting, pollution, pesticides, and, most important of all, the loss of habitat. Rain forests alone contain half the world's species of animals and plants, yet an area the size of Nebraska is being destroyed every year.

There are so many threatened animals around the world that, at the rate of one every three weeks, it would have taken Douglas and me more than three hundred years to search for them all. And if we had decided to include threatened plants as well, it would have taken another thousand years.

In every remote corner of the world there are people like Carl Jones and Don Merton who have devoted their lives to saving threatened species. Very often, their determination is all that stands between an endangered species and extinction.

But why do they bother? Does it really matter if the

Yangtze river dolphin, or the kakapo, or the northern white
rhino, or any other species live on only in scientists' note-
books?

Well, yes, it does. Every animal and plant is an integral
part of its environment: even Komodo dragons have a major
role to play in maintaining the ecological stability of their
delicate island homes. If they disappear, so could many other
species. And conservation is very much in tune with our own
survival. Animals and plants provide us with life-saving
drugs and food, they pollinate crops and provide important
ingredients for many industrial processes. Ironically, it is
often not the big and beautiful creatures, but the ugly and
less dramatic ones, that we need most.

Even so, the loss of a few species may seem almost irrelevant compared to major environmental problems such as
global warming or the destruction of the ozone layer. But
while nature has considerable resilience, there is a limit to
how far that resilience can be stretched. No one knows how
close to the limit we are getting. The darker it gets, the faster
we're driving.

There is one last reason for caring, and I believe that no
other is necessary. It is certainly the reason why so many
people have devoted their lives to protecting the likes of rhinos, parakeets, kakapos, and dolphins. And it is simply this:
the world would be a poorer, darker, lonelier place without
them.

SIFTING THROUGH THE EMBERS

HERE'S A STORY
I heard when I was young that bothered me because I
couldn't understand it. It was many years before I discovered
it to be the story of the Sybilline books. By that time all the
details of the story had rewritten themselves in my mind, but
the essentials were still the same. After a year of exploring
some of the endangered environments of the world, I think I
finally understand it.

It concerns an ancient city—it doesn't matter where it was
or what it was called. It was a thriving, prosperous city set
in the middle of a large plain. One summer, while the people
of the city were busy thriving and prospering away, a strange
old beggar woman arrived at the gates carrying twelve large
books, which she offered to sell to them. She said that the
books contained all the knowledge and all the wisdom of the

world, and that she would let the city have all twelve of them in return for a single sack of gold.

The people of the city thought this was a very funny idea. They said she obviously had no conception of the value of gold and that probably the best thing was for her to go away again.

This she agreed to do, but first she said she was going to destroy half of the books in front of them. She built a small bonfire, burnt six of the books of all knowledge and all wisdom in the sight of the people of the city, and then went on her way.

Winter came and went, a hard winter, but the city just about managed to flourish through it and then, the following summer, the old woman was back.

"Oh, you again," said the people of the city. "How's the knowledge and wisdom going?"

"Six books," she said, "just six left. Half of all the knowledge and wisdom in the world. Once again I am offering to sell them to you."

"Oh yes?" sniggered the people of the city.

"Only the price has changed."

"Not surprised."

"Two sacks of gold."

"What?"

"Two sacks of gold for the six remaining books of knowledge and wisdom. Take it or leave it."

"It seems to us," said the people of the city, "that you can't be very wise or knowledgeable yourself or you would realise that you can't just go around quadrupling an already outrageous price in a buyer's market. If that's the sort of knowledge and wisdom you're peddling, then, frankly, you can keep it at any price."

"Do you want them or not?"

"No."

"Very well. I will trouble you for a little firewood."

She built another bonfire and burnt three of the remaining books in front of them and then set off back across the plain.

That night one or two curious people from the city sneaked out and sifted through the embers to see if they could salvage the odd page or two, but the fire had burnt very thoroughly and the old woman had raked the ashes. There was nothing.

Another hard winter took its toll on the city and they had a little trouble with famine and disease, but trade was good and they were in reasonably good shape again by the following summer when, once again, the old woman appeared.

"You're early this year," they said to her.

"Less to carry," she explained, showing them the three books she was still carrying. "A quarter of all the knowledge and wisdom in the world. Do you want it?"

"What's the price?"

"Four sacks of gold."

"You're completely mad, old woman. Apart from anything else, our economy's going through a bit of a sticky patch at the moment. Sacks of gold are completely out of the question."

"Firewood, please."

"Now wait a minute," said the people of the city, "this isn't doing anybody any good. We've been thinking about all this and we've put together a small committee to have a look at these books of yours. Let us evaluate them for a few months, see if they're worth anything to us, and when you come back next year, perhaps we can put in some kind of a reasonable offer. We are not talking sacks of gold here, though."

The old woman shook her head. "No," she said. "Bring me the firewood."

"It'll cost you."

"No matter," said the woman, with a shrug. "The books will burn quite well by themselves."

So saying, she set about shredding two of the books into pieces which then burnt easily. She set off swiftly across the plain and left the people of the city to face another year.

She was back in the late spring.

"Just the one left," she said, putting it down on the ground in front of her. "So I was able to bring my own firewood."

"How much?" said the people of the city.

"Sixteen sacks of gold."

"We'd only budgeted for eight."

"Take it or leave it."

"Wait here."

The people of the city went off into a huddle and returned half an hour later.

"Sixteen sacks is all we've got left," they pleaded, "times are hard. You must leave us with something."

The old woman just hummed to herself as she started to pile the kindling together.

"All right!" they cried at last, opened up the gates of the city, and led out two ox carts, each laden with eight sacks of gold. "But it had better be good."

"Thank you," said the old woman, "it is. And you should have seen the rest of it."

She led the two ox carts away across the plain with her, and left the people of the city to survive as best they could with the one remaining twelfth of all the knowledge and wisdom that had been in the world.

Acknowledgments

We would like to thank the following people for helping to make this project possible:

Gary "Arab" Aburn
Air France
Air Zaïre
Conrad and Ros Aveling
Hilary Bass
Jane Belson
Bill Black
Boss
Juan Carlos Cardenas
John Clements
Sue Colman
Peter and Linda Daniel
Mike and Dobbie Dobbins
Phred Dobbins
Patty Eddy
Margaret Edridge
Steven Faux
John Fontana
Sue Freestone
Fuji Films
Lisa Glass
Michael Green

Reinaldo Green
Terry Greene
Linda Guess
Peter Guzzardi
Bob Harris
Bruce Harris
Rod Hay
Kes and Fraser Hillman-Smith
Craig Hodsell
Liz Jarvis
Jersey Zoo
Carl Jones
Zhou Kaiya
Aartee Khosla
Kodak UK Ltd
Jurgen Langer
Annette E. Lanjouw
Lisa Lawley
Alain le Garsmeur
Richard Lewis
Roberto Lira
London Zoo

Acknowledgments

Charles and Jane Mackie
Marina Mahon
Rob Malpas
Andrew Martin
Mark McCauslin
David McDowell
Don Merton
Doreen Montgomery
Phil Morley
Chris Muir
Nikon UK Ltd
Mary Ellen O'Neill
Bill Peabody
Chen Peixun
Susan Petersen
Jean-Jacques Petter
David Pratt
Red Cross
Liu Renjun
Marcia Ricci
Bernadette Salhi

Putra Sastrawan
Gaynor Shutte
Ivan Leiva Silva
Laurie Stark
Neville Stevenson
Wendy Strahm
Godofredo Stutzin
Miguel Stutzin
Condo Subagyo
Struan Sutherland
Kirsty Swynnerton
Debra Taylor
Ron Tindal
Tongling Baiji Conservation
   Association
Daniel Torres
Ed Victor
Sue Warner
Carlos Weber
Bob Wyatt

One More Chance...

If you would like to make a contribution to help with the conservation work for any of the animals featured in this book, please send checks payable to the organisations listed below. Don't forget to state to which project you would like the money to go.

Madagascar:

Madagascar Fund
World Wide Fund for Nature
1196 Gland, Switzerland

Indonesia:
Komodo Dragon

c/o PHPA
Jalan Suwung 40
P.O. Box 320
Denpasar, Bali
Indonesia

Zaïre:
Rhino Anti-Poaching
   Operation and Mountain
   Gorilla Project

c/o IUCN
Regional Office: Eastern Africa
P.O. Box 68200
Nairobi, Kenya

New Zealand:
Kakapo Recovery Program

c/o Threatened Species Trust
Department of Conservation
Box 10420
Wellington, New Zealand

One More Chance . . .

China:
Baiji Dolphin Conservation
    Project

c/o *People's Trust for Endangered
    Species*
Hamble House
Meadrow, Godalming
Surrey GU7 3JX
UK
or:
c/o *West Coast Whale Research
    Foundation*
P.O. Box 1768
Santa Cruz, CA 95061
USA

Mauritius:
Mauritius Wildlife Project

Mauritius Wildlife Appeal Fund
10, Dr. Ferriere Street
Port Louis, Mauritius
Indian Ocean